William Wood was born in Musselburgh Midlothian in 1943. In 1945, the family moved and settled in the town of Clackmannan. The memories of the post-war rationing years are like looking back on a completely different world when compared to today's life experience.

# William Wood

# MEMORIES OF A CLACKMANNAN LAD 1947 – 1958

AUSTIN MACAULEY PUBLISHERS™

LONDON • CAMBRIDGE • NEW YORK • SHARJAH

A CIP catalogue record for this title is available from the British Library.

ISBN 9781398479586 (Paperback)
ISBN 9781398479593 (ePub e-book)

www.austinmacauley.com

First Published 2024
Austin Macauley Publishers Ltd®
1 Canada Square
Canary Wharf
London
E14 5AA

# Table of Contents

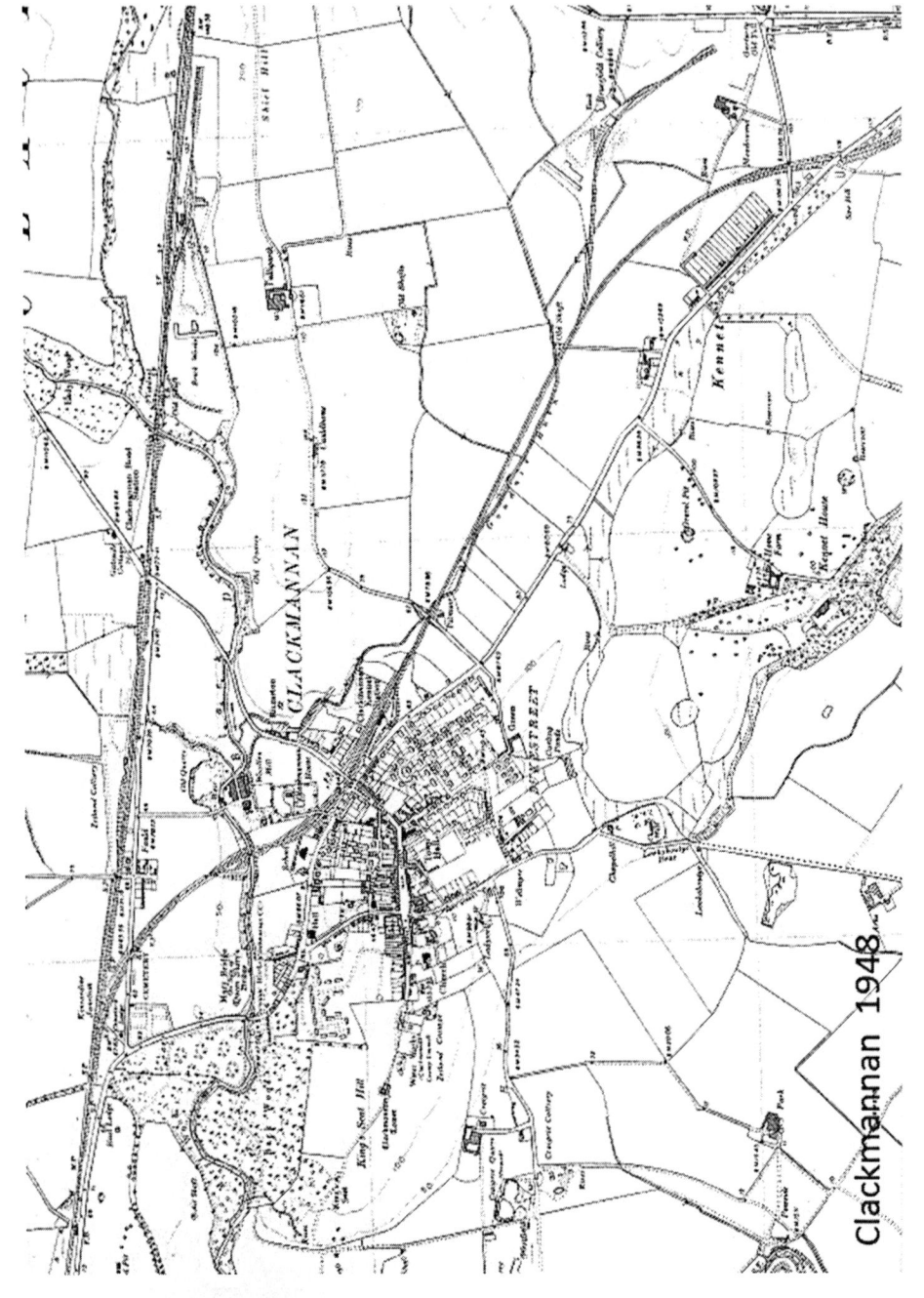

Clackmannan 1948

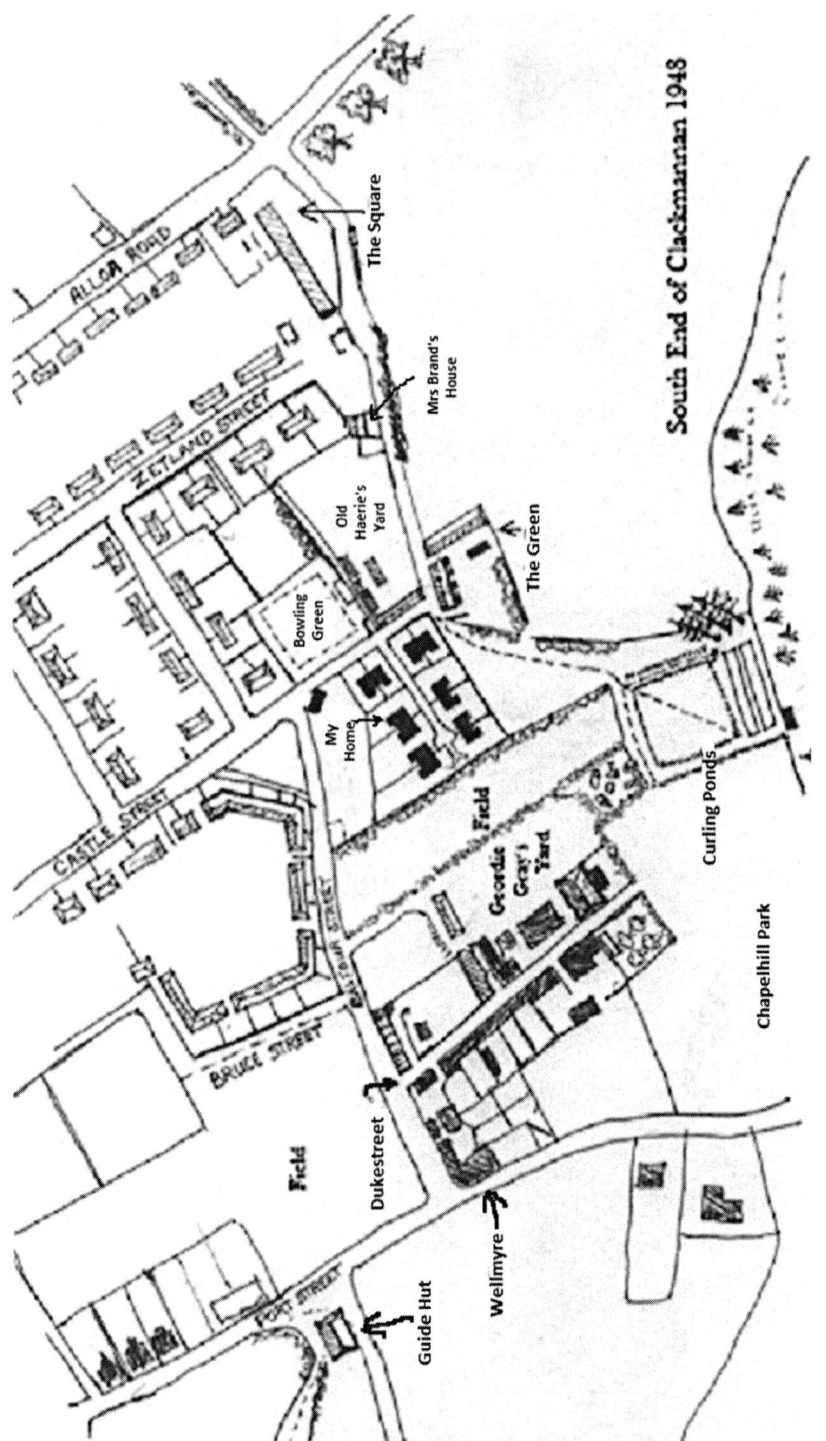

The Square

Mrs Brand's House

ALLOA ROAD

ZETLAND STREET

Old Haerie's Yard

The Green

Bowling Green

My Home

CASTLE STREET

Geordie Gray's Yard

Field

Curling Ponds

BRUCE STREET

Chapelhill Park

Dukestreet

Field

POST STREET

Wellmyre

Guide Hut

South End of Clackmannan 1948

# Introduction

An account of my childhood days in post-war Clackmannan.

I was born in my grandparents' home in Musselburgh Midlothian on 1 April 1943. In 1945, our family moved from our home in Prestonpans, East Lothian, into one of the newly built houses in Castle Terrace, Clackmannan.

Over the past few years, I began recording some of my childhood memories and eventually gave some thought to publishing the collection. The following is an account of those years during the late 1940s and ending at the start of my teens: 1958.

I have to emphasise that many of the accounts are not historically accurate; they are recollections of my childhood; dates and names of people are mostly a bit of guesswork.

The few basic sketches scattered about the pages are really only scenes of places and events that no longer exist. Also, I've included a poem at the end of the book written by a local lad, William Burns, born 1825. It's an account of his childhood days in and around the town. It struck me how similar his childhood was to my own—over 100 years before.

# Part I

# Chapter 1
# Out for a Stroll

Childhood memories are often very pleasant things, but sometimes they leave you wondering if some were merely just a dream, a figment of the imagination. One of my earliest recollections—which by the way was verified; according to my mother—was during one cold winter's day, the events of which have remained with me these past sixty odd years. World War II had ended the year before and I was just an infant, not quite four years old.

As I recall, the first thing that stirred me in the morning was the sound of my mother's voice calling us all down for breakfast. However, on that particular morning, something else prompted me to awaken earlier than usual; I'm not exactly sure what.

The first thing I encountered when I pulled back the covers was this strange ghostly glow illuminating the whole room. The source appeared to come from somewhere outside. As I reached up and peeped behind the curtain, I found the whole window completely covered in thick swirling ice crystals; apparently, the moonlight fusing with the ice caused the luminous effect.

I lay back snuggled up in bed with the blankets wrapped tightly about me, thinking of nothing in particular, just staring at the misty effect of my breath on the cold air of the room. Then for a brief moment I heard a sound, a curious intermittent murmuring. At first, thought I imagined it. I held my breath for a moment and listened … sure enough, there it was again, the faint drone of voices coming from somewhere below.

Mustering a bit of courage, I slid out from under the covers and crept down stairs. I made my way towards the kitchen, the apparent source of the sound. There I saw Ma and Dad. At first, they didn't notice me. Dad was seated on one of the kitchen chairs getting himself ready for the pit. As soon as he saw me, he smiled and said, 'Hello! What are you doing up at this time?' I sat on a chair next to him and watched the scene.

*'Hello! What are you doing up at this time?'*

He appeared to be struggling with his heavy moleskin trousers (attire specially made to deal with the rough environs of coal mining). My mother was busy making up his piece (lunch). She was, I suppose, a typical mother of that time: first one up in the morning getting everyone ready for work or school, and last to bed at night.

From the large kettle simmering gently on top of the coal-fired stove, she filled Dad's tin flask after spooning in some tealeaves. She then cut slices of crusty Co-op bread, filled them with best butter and great thick slices of cheese. All this was then packed in an ex-government gas mask bag (the type issued to service men and women during the war and ending up a very useful and popular piece-bag for workers lunches).

Dad was almost ready. After fastening the straps on his thick leather kneepads, he then filled his lamp with fresh carbide and shoved the small tin containing the remainder into his bag. He rose from the chair, kissed us all goodbye, and was soon on his way.

By the sitting room window, thawed out from the heat of the fireplace, I watched him set off through the cold morning mist. The ghostly atmosphere created by the glow of the streetlamp at the end of the Terrace added an interesting touch to the scene as dad strolled through the hazy light and drifted out of sight.

I sat for a while gazing out the window, occasionally seeing passers-by heading off to work with their overcoats and scarfs wrapped tightly about them. Then from around the corner, the familiar sound of the Co-op's electric milk float making its way from door to door, and the clinking of bottles being placed on doorsteps.

Suddenly, my reverie abruptly ended. Ma had entered the room carrying a fresh bucket of coal from the cellar. Placing the new pieces on the already lit fire caused the warmth in the room to die a little. I soon abandoned my position at the window and moved a bit closer to the fireside.

She then made her way to the bottom of the stair and called my older brother John for school. He eventually appeared and sat next to me. Moments later, my younger brother Andrew joined us, he was just a toddler, disturbing the quiet of the morning, crying for attention, and pushing his way in trying to find the most advantageous position by the fireside.

With a bowl of porridge on our laps, we eventually settled down around the hearth, transfixed by the mesmerising effect of the glowing coals.

As the morning progressed and the night sky grudgingly gave way to daylight, I ventured outside. The air was quite chilly, the cold biting my cheeks. My mother had wrapped me well in a thick jacket and large scarf that crossed over my chest and safety-pinned behind my back. The Terrace was now quite lively. Kids old enough for school were calling out to each other. My brother John eventually appeared with his school satchel strapped to his back. He joined the other kids in the Terrace, and together they all meandered up Castle Street towards the local public school. I stood there watching them, feeling a bit envious, and wishing I were old enough to join them.

The sounds of noisy youngsters soon settled down and the Terrace gradually got quieter. Just as I was about to go back in-doors, I caught sight of Mrs Mitchell; one of our neighbours who lived at No. 64 Castle Street. She was in the process of filling a bucket of coal from her cellar. I moved up towards her and asked if Emma could come out to play (Emma was the same age as me, and was Mrs Mitchell's only child at that time). She immediately answered with: 'Oh no, son! It's far too cold … maybe later.'

As she made her way back inside, I turned and moved off, ambling aimlessly along the kerbside, breaking up the thin layers of ice that had formed on all the small puddles overnight. I moved up towards the streetlamp at the corner of Castle Street and the Terrace and stood for a moment gazing out in the general direction my Dad took on his way to the Pit. I tried to imagine what it must be like; this hole in the ground they all climb down. It seemed their job was quite an adventure; making their way through endless tunnels, their small carbide lamps hooked onto their caps to guide their way. The reality of course was an environment beyond any child's imagination.

Standing at the end of the Terrace trying to picture the scene, I began to wonder just how far away the Pit was. Then, at that moment, I caught sight of auld Haerie Ferguson across the road (Haerie was just the local way of saying Harry). He was an enterprising old fellow. I believe his main occupation was a baker. He also dabbled in all sorts of various projects around his smallholding. It was like a two-acre farm with lots of hens and pigs.

The front of his property was an elongated building similar in style to Robert Burn's cottage; it ran from the bowling green down to the end of Castle Street. The dwelling part was at one end. Next-door to that was his small bake house, and next to that, the stables. The rear entrance to his smallholding was around the corner through a big timber gate. The driveway ran up to the sheds that edged the bowling green where he kept his pigs and poultry.

*Haerie Ferguson's old cottage at the end of Castle St.*

The only rear access to the dwelling part of the building was through a narrow kitchen and scullery, and at the end of the kitchen, a small doorway led into a comfortable little sitting room with a large cavity bed against the far wall. Another small doorway led to a tiny hallway giving access to the front door and master bedroom.

Although auld Haerie was always on the go with seemingly endless tasks around the place, he never the less spent most of his time in his small bake house. Often I would see him walking up the street carrying a large wooden tray full of delicious looking cakes and tarts that ended up in Dudley Hunter's general store on the corner of Castle and Balfour Street (now named Lochies Road). Even to this day, I can still picture him dressed in his long white apron, his sleeves rolled up passed his elbows, and kneading the dough with such vigour and determination.

The other thing that caught my attention was an object that stood on the inside ledge of the bake house window. It was a small paper-mashie doll in the form of a fat policeman measuring approximately ten inches in height. I can still see the shape and colour of that little fat bobby with his powder blue uniform. Each time I walked past, there he stood, his tiny fat smiling face looking down at me, his two hands clasping the large belt around his wide girth as if he were saying: *"Now then lad, move along there."*

I crossed over the road and took the opportunity of asking Haerie if he knew the whereabouts of my Dad's Pit. He glanced down at me briefly without pausing and said, 'Which one? There are four pits in the district!' He looked down at the vacant expression on my face, and then disappeared inside closing the door behind him.

After a moment or so, I turned and walked down to the end of Castle Street and stood under a gas streetlamp on the corner. From there, the road took a ninety-degree left turn down the brae towards the main road.

While standing at the corner, I looked across at an area called The Green: a small group of about a dozen single story miners' cottages. For as young as I was, I was well aware of how lucky our family was to be living in a smarter and more modern accommodation. They were a wretched looking bunch of buildings—actually, they can be seen on an old eighteenth century map of the County; I would say most certainly erected by the coal companies to accommodate the local colliers. All their amenities were outside. The toilet block was situated at the rear beside the clothes drying area. Water had to be carried in from a well at the far end. Coal for the fireplace meant a stroll round the back, and on mornings as bitterly cold as this, the task was not a particularly pleasant one. The toilet block was most likely a late addition, the previous arrangement was probably a tin box collected each week by a sewage remover.

There's an interesting comment on that subject by the Reverent Mr Robert Moodie in his contribution to the first Statistical Account of 1791. He describes the sanitary conditions in town after a severe attack of dysentery hit the parish in 1784 as follows:

*... Little care is taken to keep the streets clean. Before every door is a dunghill, on which every species of nuisance is thrown ...* (it doesn't take much to imagine the pungent aroma that drifted about town back then).

*The Green*

I was just about to turn and head home when the door of Mr Barr's house abruptly opened and a young lass appeared carrying a bucket. It was Anne. She was a year or so older than me, and in the same class as my brother John. It looked as if she was either going to be late getting to school, or she's taking the day off.

With no shoes or socks on, she ran with full speed around the corner of her house and returned shortly after with a few lumps of coal in her bucket. I attempted to ask her about Dad's pit; however, as she was wholly intent on getting back indoors out of the cold, I was given a short hurried reply, indicating that the pit was down the brae past The Square, and then she disappeared slamming the door behind her.

I stood for a moment looking at those dilapidated terraced cottages and wondered how Mr and Mrs Barr with a house full of bairns managed to cope in that small two roomed run down house.

I started off down the brae, (later to be named South Pilmuir Road) walking beside the high stonewall of auld Haerie's property, and on passed Mrs Brand's house with its very high unkempt privy hedge and large pear tree in the front garden. Just ahead of me around the bend is the entrance to Zetland Street, the home of our most formidable foe: *The Zetland Street Gang,* led by their fearless leader, Tucker Glen.

It's not exactly clear when the boys from Zetland Street and The Green became mortal enemies, but I would say it must have had its origins way back in the distant past—probably not long after Zetland Street was built; which was really only several years before the war. It may be argued that I was far too young to participate in their occasional confrontations. All I can say is that I was a loyal member of *The Green Gang,* and at this moment, I sensed a feeling of imminent danger should I be spotted anywhere near the territory of this fiendish lot.

I cautiously passed the intersection and carried on down the brae past an area the locals called The Square. The Square was at one time a group of miners' dwellings recently vacated pending demolition. Originally they stood on their own, a group of houses with a courtyard in the middle. It never occurred to me why they named this part of town The Square, there was practically nothing left of it or anything remotely resembling a square. For years after, people still called that locality *The Square,* even when all trace of it had long gone; I just accepted it.

I soon found myself standing at the edge of town, and in front of me like an unofficial boundary line where young bairns were forbidden to cross, is the main Alloa/Dunfermline road. Across on the other side, a narrow dirt road (mainly used by farm vehicles) leads down towards a humped back bridge that crosses a single line railway track, and situated beside this, a two-story semidetached house known as Pilmuir. The road then meanders up a steep brae disappearing over the other side.

I had never ventured beyond this point on my own; however, the scene did look inviting. With a little trepidation, I crossed over and set off down the rough unsealed road. A hundred yards or so further on, I reached the bridge that crossed the railway track and noticed a small stile built into a wooden fence at the side of the bridge. I climbed onto it to see where it led. Over on the other side, a well-worn footpath leads down to the edge of the railway track, and running along beside it, a small burn with the blackest looking water I had ever seen. This was the Goudnie burn. Its black colour was due to wastewater from the coal washers.

In the distance, I could see that the railway track turned off and disappeared behind a clump of Scotch Fir trees.

While standing on the stile, leaning on the top rail and taking in the scene before me, I began to sense an odd trembling sensation. Faint vibrations emanated up through the wooden stile tickling the soles of my feet. Then from somewhere behind me, a strange rumbling sound followed moments later by a couple of loud whistles. Before I had a chance to think, a steam engine suddenly burst out from under the bridge with one almighty explosion filling the air with great billowing smoke and steam. The noise gave me such a start that I fell backwards off the stile and landed on the road. Cautiously, I climbed back up and saw the train trundling along the line pulling what seemed an endless array of coal wagons. Finally, the guard wagon appeared. The guard was standing on the platform at the rear. He looked up at me and gave a wave.

*I climbed back onto the stile and waved to the guard…*

I smiled and waved back. I remember thinking at the time of what I'd give to be standing on that platform beside him.

I stood there for a while and watched the train fork off to the right. Any notion I had of descending the small pathway down to the line had all but disappeared, due to certain factors concerning my personal health and well-being. A moment or so later, I decided to press on.

The road on the other side of the bridge continued up a steep incline, and great ruts formed by rain made the walk a bit exhausting. When I eventually reached the top of the brae, I paused for a moment to catch my breath. As I stood looking out at the surrounding countryside, one of our County's most spectacular sights immediately caught my attention. There, spread out before me was a magnificent unobstructed view of the Ochil Hills, their peaks covered in pristine snow. The sight was quite breath-taking.

I stood there for some time just taking in the surrounding district. Our town looked especially picturesque with all the houses resting on the slope of a small rise. Standing out among the cluster of houses, I could see quite clearly the unmistakable features of our church tower, and a little to the right, perched on the very top of the rise, the historical tower of Clackmannan. It was said that Robert the Bruce had it built as a hunting lodge; however, the story has never been confirmed. Certainly, the view from up on the Tower Brae is quite impressive. Often, while on walks up there with my dad, we would see large coal ships from foreign parts steaming up the River Forth heading for the Alloa dock. Then there were the constant presence of mud dredgers moving slowly up and down the river keeping the channels clear.

Just to the left of town is Kennet village with its single row of stone terraced cottages, and opposite them is the Kennet Estate where at this moment, the late morning sun is just above the horizon, its warmth hindered by the cold haze, and white ground frost still evident in places not yet exposed by it. Then, almost obscured amidst a group of oak and chestnut trees, I could just make out the distinctive shape of Kennet farm with its Tuscan style light brown terra cotta roof tiles. A short distance further up, Kennet House, former residence of Alexander Hugh Bruce the 6th Lord Balfour of Burleigh; which we aptly named, *The Big Hoose*.

According to the Rev Mr Robert Moodie in the 1791 Statistical Account, the house was completed in circa 1790 and was designed by a Mr Harrison of

Lancaster. The Rev Robert went on at great lengths describing its charms and beauty … it certainly did contribute to the already pleasing landscape.

Access to the estate is a short distance along the main road from The Square. From this vantage point, there is a clear view of the gatehouse lodge with its interesting curved wall. The locals call it, *The Blue House*. I can picture the gateman in years gone by tipping his hat as the gentry in their coaches passed through the big gates. The coaches would then make their way up the winding road edged with large clumps of Rhododendron bushes, and on through the beautiful wooded parkland of oaks, poplars, and chestnut trees. When arriving at the great entrance, they were most likely greeted by the butler or footman.

*Kennet House…*

When the 6th Lord Balfour died in 1921, the family moved a few years later into Brucefield House and leased the Kennet estate to various tenants. By 1946, the Alloa Co-operative purchased most of the estate. The produce from the market gardens ended up on the Co-op shelves, and the mansion was subdivided into rental apartments. It would be some years later that I would get the opportunity to pay regular visits to the interior of this great house. I delivered the Sunday newspapers to each of the occupants.

It was actually quite a pleasant way to spend a Sunday morning: cycling off towards Kennet village, and on through the Kennet estate. However, there was just one small problem on entering the mansion. One of the tenants owned a very big *'hound of the Baskerville'* type dog, and as I entered the main hallway, it stirred itself into action. Fortunately, the entrance hall being quite spacious with a glossy granite floor played a useful part in dealing with the situation. I would move a few paces in, and as it came bounding towards me, I would then quickly step to one side. It slid along the smooth granite floor giving me enough time to enter the next doorway. The same action would happen again as I left the building. This plan was demonstrated to every newsboy on that particular delivery.

While I stood looking down the brae at this angle, I found I now had an unobstructed view of the railway line. I could also see quite clearly the town's railway station with its old Victorian style ticket office and waiting room. Over to the left, as the line passed the group of Scotch Fir trees near the spot where the train had turned earlier, I noticed a group of industrial looking buildings … was that my dad's pit?

As I stood for a few moments contemplating the scene, I inadvertently turned and caught sight of another group of similar buildings about half a mile away on the other side of the field directly behind me. They seemed a lot closer and more accessible; also, the going was not so rough, and a gradual downhill slope all the way. I set off at a steady pace towards them.

Just ahead, about a hundred yards along the way, I noticed a small group of farm worker's cottages. Some infants were playing nearby. At the rear of the cottages, a couple of women were hanging cloths on a rope line. As soon as the kids caught sight of me, they stopped their play. The presence of a stranger— especially one as young as I was—must have looked a little bit unusual. They just stood there watching me approach, their faces showing no expression. I began to feel a bit uneasy. I looked straight ahead and kept walking. Suddenly, a tiny voice broke the uneasy silence with the enquiry: 'What's your name?' This took me completely by surprise. I turned and faced my inquisitor; a bright precocious looking individual wrapped in a colourful coat and scarf. She wore a woollen *Pixie* bonnet that covered her ears and came to a point at the back of her head. The bonnet gave her face a mischievous look, and her smile was quite infectious.

I replied shyly: 'My name's Billy.' She chattered on at some length. Her Dad apparently works at Mr Norvall's farm just a short distance down the road. When they finally asked me where I was going, I explained that my Dad was a coalminer, and I just wanted to see where he works. I told them that I was heading for the group of buildings at the end of the road. One of the lads then said that the place was actually the Cherryton Brick Works. He wasn't sure about the coal mine. Then the other lad joined in and said that there is a pit further down on the other side of the slagheap next to the brickworks.

*'What's your name?'*

This made me a bit apprehensive and I began to wonder if maybe I should give up the whole idea and head back home. After a moment or so, I thought … well, I've come this far, I might as well take a look at the brickworks; maybe somebody there knows something about a pit. So, I said cheerio to my new pals and headed off down the road passed Mr Norvall's farm, finally arriving at the spot where the farm road joined a 'B' class sealed road.

I crossed over towards the nearest building. On the road directly in front of it lay a huge metal plate that wobbled when I walked over it; it was actually the scales for weighing the lorries. There didn't seem to be anyone about, so I wandered over towards a long brick building that stretched all the way down towards a railway embankment. The structure stood about ten or twelve feet in height, and along each side, spaced evenly apart, were small doorways. From these doorways, men appeared pushing barrow loads of bricks.

Walking along the side of it, I noticed that some of the doorways were almost completely bricked up. As I moved a bit closer, I immediately felt a tremendous heat radiating from them. Each bricked up doorway had a small inspection hole, and at a safe distance, I could see something that resembled a scene of what hell must be like. Emanating from the tiny gap was a white-hot wavering glow. I could feel the heat around my very eyes. What I was witnessing was the process of raw clay bricks being baked in hot ovens.

I stood there for a few minutes enjoying the warmth and watching the men go about their work, wheeling freshly cut brown coloured clay into the ovens, and removing the finished product. They appeared to be too busy performing their task to take any notice of me. Actually, I rather got the impression that perhaps maybe I was in the way. Eventually, I wandered back towards the road.

*The Cherryton Brickworks…*

Just outside the office, I noticed a man sitting on a bench near the doorway. He sat with his back against the wall, his legs stretched out in front of him and smoking a white clay pipe. He wore a wide brimmed skip bonnet and an old black suit that obviously had seen better days, and every now and then, he would pull the pipe out of his mouth and give a good spit. His face gave away no expression as he watched me approach. I stood awkwardly before him.

Making my enquiries, I waited for a response. He just sat there sucking on his pipe. Finally, he muttered something like: 'What's your name son?' I think I replied with the usual three-year-old response and said: 'My name's Billy!'

Unable to get my full name, he gave up. Gesturing with his pipe, he pointed along the road and said, 'The old pit head is just down there.'

It was the grimmest looking stretch of road I had ever seen. Immediately on my left was this huge intimidating mound of waste material formed by years of mining, and running along the other side of the road, thick gorse bushes covered with grey dust; a result of heavy trucks splashing mud on them during wet days. About a hundred yards along and just around the curve in the road, there it stood, the Tulligarth Pit; actually, no longer being worked underground. However, there were still a small group of surface workers; probably maintenance men.

One of the structures immediately caught my attention. It was the shape of a very large iron tripod, and at the top of this, a big wheel. The bottom half was covered with corrugated iron, and at the front, a small doorway. I made my way towards it. The noise coming from this building was excruciating. I slowly, and with great caution, opened the door and stepped inside. It was not a pleasant place to be. The whole layout of the interior was a mass of iron beams. There were no constructed floors or ceilings, just iron stairs leading to ramps, and the noise was unrelenting.

From above, I heard a man's voice calling out to me. As I looked up, I could see he was already making his way down a vertical iron ladder. He approached me and after a brief greeting, I tried to express the purpose of my visit. He took me into a small area where there were already two or three others sitting about, presumably having their lunch break. I remember being given a tin mug full of hot black tea. I tried a sip and quickly found it to be very bitter, and far too hot. There must have been a bit of a discussion between them, for it seemed that one of the men had been elected to take me to a higher authority.

At the end of their break, the elected fellow escorted me across the yard towards a small rectangular flat roofed brick building with white painted exterior walls. As soon as we stepped inside, I was immediately presented to an important looking gentleman dressed in a suit, a gold fob watch chain hung from his waste-coat, and in the corner of his mouth, a large brown pipe. His name was Mr McGhie, the mine manager.

The man who brought me patted me on the head and left. I turned to confront the important looking gentleman sitting at his desk. Mr McGhie took a couple of puffs from his pipe, looked straight at me with a mild curious expression, then rose from his chair and propped himself on the edge of his desk. Taking in a couple of extra puffs from his pipe, he finally said something like: 'Well, what are we going to do with you, eh?'

After a pause, he turned to address someone behind him. As he stepped aside, there, sitting by a warm potbelly stove was a large figure of a man dressed all in black. On the desk next to him lay a black peek hat with black and white checks around the rim. I was face to face with none other than PC Meldrum, the local bobby.

*'Well, what are we going to do with you, eh?'*

The questions now seemed to take on a more serious note, beginning with, what is my name, and who are my parents, etc.

Finally, he got up from his chair, and as he rose, I remember thinking at the time how big he was, this towering creature all dressed in black. He took me by the hand and led me outside, picking up his bicycle on the way.

In the course of walking back along the farm road towards town, PC Meldrum did his best to keep me amused. When I asked him if he caught many bad people, and what did he do with them when he did, he decided to demonstrate by using me as a culprit. From his back pocket, he took out a pair of handcuffs and promptly fitted them around my small wrists. We then continued on our way, acting out the scene of the captive criminal.

As we approached the farm workers cottages, I saw no sign of the kids. Suddenly, from around the corner, a woman appeared carrying a basket of cloths from her washing line. She greeted us with a warm hello, and with cheery humour said, 'I see you've apprehended a villain, PC Meldrum!' He replied with equally humorous banter, 'Oh, Aye! He put up quite a struggle, but we managed to catch him in the end … etc.' Then from the doorway, the youngsters appeared. I gave them a wave. I must say, I suddenly felt a wee bit silly.

We made our way down the steep brae towards the humpback bridge. Then in the distance, I saw a familiar figure walking over the bridge. It was my mother, and trailing along beside her, my younger brother Andrew. I had obviously caused some concern at home. Even from some distance off, I could detect that my mother's voice had an overly anxious tone.

*PC Meldrum released me to my mother's care…*

As we met up, PC Meldrum decided not to press charges, and released me to her care. When I explained the purpose of my mission, she just turned and pointed in the direction of the Scotch Firs along the railway line and said, 'Your Dad works over there in Brucefield, he'll be home in a few hours.'

On the way home, I was lectured about the dangers of a small child wandering off beyond the precincts of home, and I was made to promise never to do such a thing again … of course, I agreed.

Later that afternoon, as John arrived home from school, we went outside to play before tea. Moments later, Ma came out and called John saying, 'Why don't you take Billy down to the bridge, and wait for your Dad coming home from the pit?'

Darkness on that early winter's evening had already descended as we made our way down towards the bridge. I stood on the wooden fence looking out along the line. A few minutes later, I saw in the distance the flicker of a tiny light, then another, and another, and soon there were scores of bright shining dots from carbide lamps bobbing from side to side as the miners made their way home along the railway track.

About five or so minutes later, the first of them ascended the pathway from the railway track and climbed over the small wooden stile. I called out occasionally when I thought I recognised Dad, but it was difficult, not only because of the darkness, but also because this was in the days before the pits had baths. All the miners came home with their faces covered in coal dust.

Then from a short distance off, I heard the familiar sound of his voice. As he climbed up onto the stile, I called out. I will always remember that moment. His teeth appeared so white behind his coal black face. As I walked home beside my Dad, I thought to myself, every day should be an adventure.

# Chapter 2
# School Days

The animals on the ceiling pranced about from one corner to the other. They were a strange collection of giraffes, donkeys and teddy bears. Their movements appeared slow as if floating across the surface of the moon, and through it all, the sound of echoic voices, low, almost whispering. Then gradually, I became aware of a dark figure looming over me, an unfamiliar face dressed in shirt, tie and jacket; and around his neck hung an odd tube-like device, the end of which searched my chest as if listening for something.

A second figure appeared from just behind him. I recognised him at once. It was Dad. Both were looking down at me and talking quietly to each other. I couldn't quite make-out what was going on. Then the bedroom door gently opened and my mother appeared. She looked down at me with a concerned smile. A few seconds later I drifted off, back to join the animals on the ceiling.

Apparently, I was struck down with an acute ear infection. The illness was quite a strange experience. I was already several weeks late for the start of school. Then one morning, my mother decided I was fit enough and got me ready for my first day.

*We entered the playground through large wrought iron gates…*

With my brand new school satchel slung over my back, we strode off hand in hand through the town towards the Public School. We entered the playground through large wrought iron gates, and made our way amidst the throngs of noisy infants towards the main entrance. My mother took me directly to the headmaster's office, and finally I was deposited in a classroom on my own. I was given a pot of paint, a brush, and some sheets of newspaper. I splashed the paint around creating a row of trees—I don't know why I chose trees as a subject; perhaps I just found the basic shapes easy.

Before too long, I heard the sound of a bell. The noise out in the playground gradually died down. Eventually, the clatter of feet could be heard along the corridor, and seconds later, the classroom door suddenly swung open.

The first to greet me was a small bright face young lad with prominent ears. I recognised him at once. His name was George Solomon, a member of the notorious Zetland Street Gang. All the other five year olds in the town soon followed him, and then moments later the teacher appeared. She was a youngish lady with thick-rimmed spectacles and dark well-groomed hair. Her presence caused a sudden change in the atmosphere, and the silence that followed was a bit intimidating. She greeted us with: 'Good morning, children!' The whole class replied in unison: 'Good morning Miss!'

She began by introducing me to the rest of the class, and as she did so, she picked up my scrap of paper with the painted trees. I got the impression she quite liked my effort. She then showed me to a vacant seat right next to George. There we sat, side-by-side, each of us members of two opposing gangs who were constantly at war with each other. However, all feelings of apprehension soon ebbed due to his cheerful nature.

As I settled in, I noticed that George wasn't the only rival gang member. There were several others. All of us sitting in the same classroom ... my education was about to begin.

After a few weeks, our classroom activities settled down to a tedious routine. The thing I had looked forward to for so long was beginning to be a bit disappointing; in fact, I was fast becoming bored with the whole experience. I did enjoy one little break where we were given toys to play with. There were things like coloured cubes with letters of the alphabet painted on them, and wooden steam engines. The girls had doll-houses and toy cups and saucers. I remember there was one favourite toy that we all hoped to get our hands on before the others. The problem was getting to it first without causing a riot in front of the teacher. It was a small wooden castle with knights on horseback. But, all too soon, the short break was over and it was back to the same routine.

I caught myself daydreaming a number of times especially during certain subjects. There was never a problem with learning words or numbers; in fact, I was quite good at picking up the basics. I think it must have been the shear repetitiveness of the whole schooling experience.

There was another aspect to this new life that gave me some concern ... school discipline. Never before had I come across grown-ups who inflicted random amounts of physical pain upon children so young. It seemed to be the same few who were picked on constantly. As for the rest of us, we simply cowered in fear, wondering when our turn would come. The leather strap across the palm of the hand for the smallest misdemeanour was the most common punishment. However, one or two were thrashed in the most hideous fashion.

We were only a few weeks into the first term when one morning the teacher had the whole class standing in a semi-circle in front of the black board. All we had to do was recognise the numbers from zero to nine. She called our names in turn and pointed to a number on the blackboard. One unfortunate lad just couldn't get it. Young Ian Glen, nicknamed *Guinea* (because his face apparently resembled the look of a Guinea Pig). He was thrown to the floor and brutally kicked in front of the whole class. One wee lassie burst into tears with the shock.

Another very unpleasant incident happened sometime later. George, the lad I met on the first day, began to rebel. The rest of us just sat frozen to our chairs and watched the whole scene develop. He began by bravely challenging the teacher, and refusing to carry out one of her instructions. When she responded by threatening him with the strap, he suddenly let go with a mouthful of oaths. She just stood there looking at the lad for several seconds, her mouth wide open and her spectacles dropping to the end of her nose. She momentarily looked at the rest of us, and then abruptly left the room.

We all started looking at each other, and then at young George. He just smiled at us with his arms folded as if to say: *"That's the way to deal with that problem."*

*Headmaster taking wee Geordie away for a guid lethering…*

The murmuring in the class increased. We all began talking to each other. Several minutes had passed when suddenly the door swung open. Standing there in the doorway was the headmaster, a big six-foot creature with the meanest look on his face; traces of blood dotted his chin due to small shaving nicks. He immediately grabbed George and dragged him out of the classroom screaming. The teacher closed the door and continued as if that was the end of the matter.

George's screams could be heard all over school. We sat in our seats petrified. A few minutes later, there was silence. Then after about half an hour, the classroom door opened and the headmaster appeared with George. He was given a warning and told to go back to his seat.

For the rest of the day, he just sat staring down at his desk. I was half expecting to see some signs of physical marks or bruises, but there was nothing. It wasn't until next day that we heard what happened.

He apparently was dragged along the corridor to the cloakroom area, forcibly held over one of the wash-hand basins and a bar of soap thrust into his mouth (the headmaster's particular method of cleansing bad language from the mouths of young infants). His mouth was then kept closed for a few seconds, after which, he was placed across the headmaster's knee and thoroughly thrashed. He was then detained in the headmaster's office until eventually he calmed down.

Weeks and months passed without much happening. The initial feeling of boredom eventually transcended into an acceptable level. Most of us gradually adapted to the new conditions. The odd smack across the palm of our hand by the teacher's leather strap had to some degree evolved into a norm of school life. Another form of punishment was being dragged out by the scruff of the neck and paraded in front of the class; a humiliating penalty for not paying attention.

*My sketch of a Huckleberry Finn raft…*

Each weekend was eagerly looked forward to. I would sit at my desk planning the weekend's activities. Drawing on scraps of paper, plans for my secret hideaway, or more ambitious projects like a *Huckleberry Finn* raft … with perhaps a cabin secured to the middle of the deck … and maybe a pole attached to the roof of the cabin, and even a small sail fitted. There was no limit to the imagination. Sailing down the Black Devon River and through the uncharted and hostile depths of the Back Wood; winding my way around the unfamiliar bends and on to who knows where. Quite often, my reverie would be interrupted by a piece of chalk thrown at me by the teacher in an attempt to bring me back down to earth.

As a child, I was very quiet, hardly spoke, and as a result, was frequently described by teachers as *not very bright; a dreamer*. This didn't bother me unduly. Chastisement was like anything else at school. One soon adapted to the regime. I was by no means the only poor sod getting it. There were quite a number of us at the bottom end of the class.

Most of the lassies on the other hand were a different kettle of fish. They took to the life as all part of the grand scheme of things. They were forever bringing the teacher wee gifts: a posy of wild flowers from the neighbouring estates, the odd apple or orange, and in certain cases sweets—which in those early days of post wartime rationing demonstrated an uppishness very few could match.

Different behavioural patterns between the lassies and us were becoming increasingly apparent. Their unwillingness to join in on the most minor misdemeanour, and their disappointing habit of informing the teacher of our particular transgressions left us with no alternative but to declare the entire sex quite untrustworthy.

As infants, we shared the lassies' playground until reaching the advanced age of seven where we were then transferred to the boys' section. The lassies' playground activities consisted of skipping rope, ball games and dance routines, generally accompanied with various rhythmic chanting of verses and short songs. Their obvious talent in this field of activity was quite remarkable.

We boys, on the other hand, played competitive sports; mainly soccer, touch-tag, or some other them-and-us game. Cowboys and Indians were among the most popular at that time. The various assortment of out-buildings in the playground provided interesting little nooks and crannies to stimulate the imagination. For example, the small narrow passageway between the perimeter wall and the dining hall was frequently used for ambushing the Dillon Gang, or those dastardly outlaws of the Hopalong Cassidy and Roy Rogers films.

Then there were the two air-raid shelters. One situated at the far corner of the playground and the other behind the main building, kept permanently locked. They were featureless rectangular brick buildings with flat roofs, a door at each end, and of course no windows. The older boys' playground also had a couple. I don't know if there were any occasions to use them. I suppose the odd stray bomb may have been a possibility.

There was—so we were told—an incident with a German bomber shot down over Kennetpans, about a mile or so down the Carse. Some people said that the tail of the aeroplane could be seen sticking out the muddy banks of the River Forth several years after. Apparently, one of the crew survived. Some of the locals even remember him being transported on the back of an army lorry and taken to the Drill Hall in North Street before being shipped off to a prisoner of war camp.

After the war, most of the POWs returned to their homeland, but some remained. Two of them chose to settle in our town after the war. Neil (Neillie) Grasso, (who—I was told later—was not actually a POW but an Italian foreign national held in detention during the conflict) he opened a small fish and chip shop at the top end of Main Street where the present entrance gate to the church is now situated. It was known as *The Tower Café*. His popular servings of 'chips and peas' earned a reputation among the locals for their flatulent consequences. The dish subsequently became known around the district as *Neillie's Chips and Farters*. Some years later, he built himself a fine purpose built fish & chip restaurant in Castle Street with accommodation above it. He and his wife Florence (Flo) had two bairns; a boy and a girl (Remo and Vilma). Neillie ended up one of the most respected citizens of our town.

The other young man, commonly referred to as *Joe the Gerry*, worked on the local farms. He was a very quiet man, hardly ever heard him utter a word. It was many years later, while in my teens that I first spoke to him. I asked him what region of Germany he came from. 'Munich,' was his reply.

One day, the old janitor of our school carelessly left the door of the No.2 air raid shelter wide open. The dark interior was instantly transformed into a mysterious forbidding place where only the very brave would venture. The dares expressed by each of us were never taken up. We could only guess what hideous end would befall any young kid who entered that dark passageway. To this day, the interior of those dark dank buildings remain a mystery. Hard to imagine what it might have been like if the air-raid siren had sounded. The thought of all those youngsters and teachers piling into that claustrophobic little space is too awful to imagine.

Directly opposite the No.1 air raid shelter on the far corner of the playground stood the small drill hall, used mainly for general school gatherings, and some

PT classes. The older lads of St Mungo's Catholic school in Alloa also used the hall for their woodwork lessons. A dozen or so woodwork benches were stacked neatly down the far end of the hall and every now and then, we caught a glimpse of the lads coming and going. Being a catholic in our town seemed to involve a whole lot of travelling. They also had to take the bus into Alloa for their Sunday Church services. In comparison, it seemed we had everything on our doorstep.

Occasionally, our local Presbyterian Church Minister, Dr Crouther Gordon, would call into our school for a short talk. He was—it seemed to me—a very distinguished looking man with a good sense of dress. His suits were always immaculate, and seemed to match his spotless dog-collar and blue vest. I always enjoyed the sound of his voice. It was quite different from the vigorous authoritative voices of our teachers. It had a quality of compassion and sincerity that seemed to appeal to us youngsters. The whole school would gather in the hall and listen to his stories. They were generally tales of a religious nature, but quite often, they were talks of local interest.

One particular time he spoke of a small burn in the district, a burn that contained fragments of gold. We sat around on the old Baltic Pine floor listening to the tale with hypnotic fascination. From his coat pocket, he produced a small glass jar full of black river silt and instructed the child nearest him to pass it round. Sure enough, there through the glass and contrasting with the black silt, were tiny specks of yellow. This was truly fascinating stuff; right here on our doorstep, the very thing that old Gabby Hayes with his pack mules struggled to find in the High Sierras during those occasional screenings at the Gaumont picture house. I was primed and eager for more information. The small burn he mentioned was the Goudnie. It runs past the Brucefield coalmine, and under the humped back bridge at Pilmuir, then into the Black Devon River near the Riccarton.

Dr Gordon then enlightened us to the fact that the actual name Goudnie, is in fact an old Scottish word meaning gold. He went on to explain that separating the gold from the mud would be an extremely tedious affair, and certainly not worth the bother. This of course did not deter me from further investigation at the earliest opportunity.

After school, I headed off in the general direction of the Goudnie burn only to discover that a few of my schoolmates had the same idea. We ran to the spot down past the Riccarton and hit the banks, scrapping away with our bare hands, shoving and pushing each other for the best spots. It didn't take long to get fed up with the sheer futility of our enterprise.

One by one, we drifted off home with our school satchels dragging along the ground, and our good school cloths covered in muddy black silt. No matter how hard I tried to explain and get my mother enthused about the gold story, she just wasn't in the mood. My clothes were immediately whipped off me, the large washtub in the scullery was filled with hot water, and I was promptly dumped in and scrubbed from head to foot. As my school clothes were the only decent things I possessed, they too were given a scrub and hung in front of the fire.

## The Weekend Finally Arrives

I loved my bed. Lying in until nine and ten o'clock seemed perfectly natural. I could never understand, even to this day, why *morning-people* feel the need to censure that particular little treat. Their reproaches generally take the form: *You are wasting the best part of the day; early to bed, early to rise; the early bird etc, etc, etc....*

Of course, there were the odd occasions when I would get up before dawn. For example, that particular morning a year or so before when I set off looking for my Dad's Pit; but that was not my typical trait. I'm just one of those people who spend most of the morning gradually *coming-to;* so therefore, Saturday and Sunday mornings spent in bed were treasured.

Eventually, I would rise and make my way down stairs to greet the rest of the family. Our breakfasts were typically a piece of toast or porridge with a dollop of homemade raspberry or bramble jam in the middle (if there was one thing good that came out of the war and rationing years, it was making people aware of all the natural produce lying about the countryside. My mother's homemade bramble jam went down a treat).

After breakfast, I would sit about the house for a while, and then eventually wander off to play with my pals. Hanging about the house too long often had its downside. My mother was one of those people who didn't appreciate idleness. Eventually, there would be a request for some little task; usually an errand to one of the local shops. More often than not, it would be a visit to Jean Forsyth's general store at the top of the Cattle Market to fetch a supply of carbide for Dad's pit lamp, or taking the radio accumulator to be recharged (due to our previous home having only gas and no electrical connection, our first radio could only operate with batteries).

The accumulator, for example, was an oblong shaped glass jar, a little bigger than a jam jar containing acid. Its main purpose was to provide low voltage to the radio valves. The radio also had two other batteries that needed replacing periodically. The large high-tension battery, about the size of a thick telephone book, and a smaller one called the grid-leak; an odd looking battery with lots of holes in it where tiny plugs could be pushed in to vary voltage levels. When I think back on it now, the early radios seemed a very complicated affair (having said that, modern computers are a bit of a headache with all their cables and attachments). However, it wasn't long before we had a more modern mains powered set that plugged directly into the wall.

The radio plays and comedy sketches were of course my favourite: *Dick Barton Special Agent;* Jimmy Logan and Molly Weir; Jimmy Edwards in *Take It From Here; The Glums* or Peter Brough the ventriloquist, with his dummy Archie Andrews (it never occurred to me until years later how the BBC had the audacity to present a ventriloquist act on radio).

Later in the afternoon, if there happened to be a good film showing at one of the picture-houses in Alloa, Ma would cart us all off to see it, while Dad got himself ready for another session around the domino table at Nan Connacher's Horse Shoe Bar in the Main Street.

The Saturday night trips to the cinemas in Alloa were, for us, an exciting event, especially during the days before television. The town was filled with the sounds of people enjoying the weekend break from the drudgery of the working day. The long daylight hours of summer contrasted with the dark winter months displaying brightly lit shops, and the flashing intermittent lights from cinemas with their illuminated billboards showing the scenes of the current film. The length of the queues outside the cinemas depended on the popularity of the film.

Each picture house employed a decoratively dressed door attendant with a peak cap, a long maroon coat with yellow epaulettes on the shoulders, braided cuffs and white gloves. He looked a splendid figure, maintaining order in the ranks, allowing just so many at a time to approach the ticket booth.

When our turn eventually came, we walked through the main swing doors, passed the ticket booth, and entered a world of plush wall-to-wall carpets, glittering chandeliers, and a buffet that sold tubs of Wall's ice cream, Smith's potato crisps and cordials. Then, passing through another series of doorways, we entered the grand auditorium where we sat waiting to be transported into a magical world of adventure.

After the show, we were treated to a bag of chips at the Mar Café and maybe a black pudding supper to be shared between us. Then finally, the bus home. A quick cup of cocoa and off to bed.

## A Sunday Stroll

Now, it seems that I was forever wandering off on my own causing my mother a great deal of stress and worry. Groups of kids would be recruited and sent off in all directions looking for me. One particular adventure, I recall, occurred due to a series of unrelated circumstances. It all started when I had a kind of fixation about an old Victorian wrought iron footbridge that crossed the main Alloa/Dunfermline railway line. I would catch a glimpse of it from the bus window while accompanying my mother on one of her shopping trips to Alloa. The curious fascination this old bridge had for me is a bit difficult to explain. Maybe its imposing shape caught my attention, or that having such an elaborate structure in—what seemed to me—a remote place.

Situated just beside it were level crossing gates and a small cottage; most likely accommodation for the British Rail employee, his principle task being to operate the gates when requested by whoever. Perhaps the other attraction it had for me was the view it offered. It being a footbridge meant that it was like a narrow platform over the actual railway line, and the gaps in the iron handrails gave an unobstructed view of the trains passing underneath. My mind was made up, as soon as the first opportunity presented itself, I would take a closer look.

It was a Sunday morning, the Sunday Post arrived an hour or so before, and the latest adventures of *Oor Wullie* and *The Broons* had already been consumed. The solitary bell peeling from the church could now be heard all over town. People on the streets (the majority were women, dressed in their finest) were making their way to hear yet another eloquent sermon by our Rev Dr Crouther Gordon; and on such a beautiful sunny morning, the last thing on my mind was that bridge.

Dad was already in his garden tending the rows of cabbages and tatties, and drifting in the air, the sound of bumblebees as they flitted over the Sweet William and Lilac bushes that lined the side fence. It seemed that God indeed was in his heaven, and all was well in The Terrace.

I stood watching Dad for a few moments; contemplated the idea of assisting him with a bit of weeding, or some other such task; but I quickly abandoned the notion—I never did like gardening. There was the odd occasion when I made the attempt in order to earn an extra penny or two to buy one of Lizzy Gardner's toffee apples, but more often than not, I gave up half way through the job.

I meandered off over the back garden fence into what was once a 1½-acre plot of waste land belonging to auld Haerie Ferguson. Some of the older boys in town used it as a football pitch, using their jackets or jerseys as goal posts. Occasionally, groups of Fairground people would arrive with their colourful trucks and richly decorated caravans. They'd form a circle around the edge of the field and assemble their stalls and merry-go-rounds in the centre. It was quite an exciting event, illuminated with hundreds of electric-light bulbs flashing in the evening air, the constant sound of windpipe music, and crowds of people moving about from stall to stall. My favourites were the dodgem cars and the merry-go-round, and then finally, as my allowance reached the end, I'd chance my luck on rolling the last of my pennies at the penny-a-pitch stall in an attempt to win enough for one more go at something … I never did succeed.

Crossing the waste ground and standing at the edge of Balfour Street, (now called Lochies Road) I suddenly took the notion of paying a call on my pal Jackie. We got to really know each other after the teacher had us sit together during a kind of classroom reshuffle. I must say, the first time I met him I was a bit apprehensive.

It was about a year or so before when I was playing by myself in the waste ground at the rear of our house. I came across this young lad making all sorts of grunting noises. He kept pulling up tufts of grass and throwing them at me. He was actually going through basic animal threatening gestures similar to a disgruntled Chimpanzee. I thought at the time he had a bit of a want—to use one of my mother's expressions. Anyway, it's amazing how quickly bairns get over minor setbacks.

When I first met Jackie, I apparently had a wee problem with his surname. Somehow or other, his mother's maiden name got mentioned (the name was Dalrymple). When my mother asked me what the name of my new pal was, it seemed I had a wee bit of difficulty pronouncing it and ended up calling him Jackie Plum. From that moment on, Jackie was always known in our family by that pseudonym.

I made my way towards his house, knocked on the front door, and moments later his Granny appeared. She was already on her way out to join the others for the Sunday service. I never knew quite what to make of old Mrs Dalrymple, she came out with the oddest expressions, something to do with devils, burning fires, and eternal damnation … a wee bit on the deep side for a five year old.

A few weeks before, I apparently caused a minor scandal when the old lady was informed that I didn't wear underpants. I still don't know to this day why my mother never considered providing us with that particular item of clothing, perhaps it was due to the cloths rationing. Whatever the reason, old Mrs Dalrymple assured me I was destined for *The Burning-Fire*; my fate was sealed, there would be no mercy. (Her greatest mentor and devotee was the American evangelist, Billy Graham. She was forever going on about his great deeds and immaculate wisdom.)

However, on this meeting I was informed that Jackie had gone to Stirling with his mother visiting relatives, and that he would not be back for quite some time, and with that, she closed the door behind her and hurried off to join the other ladies on their way to church.

Standing at the front gate, watching old Mrs Dalrymple and her friends making their way up Castle Street, I decided—without any real purpose—to move off in that general direction. I passed old Mr Dunlop's big house at the top of the brae and lingered for a moment at Lizzy Gardner's tuck shop window. I stood there gazing in at the goods on display. There wasn't much; not just because the area around her display window was so tiny, but that wartime rationing was still imposed on certain goods … sweeties.

Every now and then, there would be toffee apples on display. They would be placed on a shallow baking tray to cool. This gave the top of the apples a flat layer of toffee that looked like a schoolmaster's mortarboard. Lizzy probably made them from her own supply of sugar. She may even have got the apples from old Mr Dunlop's garden next door … actually, my own mother was a dab hand at making toffee. If she found herself with a little extra sugar left over, she'd mix up a batch. The hot toffee would then be placed out on the window ledge to cool. The time it took for that toffee to harden seemed eternal. Anyway, Lizzy's shop was closed … probably gone to church … in any case, I had no money.

I moved off, strolling along Castle Street towards Main Street. On the right at No.11 is the McAinsh family farmyard. As I approached the opening to the yard, I noticed Wullie McAinsh in the process of feeding his pigs. While standing there watching him, I suddenly spotted Mat Hogan coming out of his place across the road at No.10. I didn't know it at the time until much later that he was actually a prisoner of war. He was captured near Dunkirk in 1940 and spent the rest of the war in a POW camp somewhere in Germany. Apparently, there were quite a few of the lads from Clackmannan in the same situation: Rob McLelland from Craigrie Terrace; George Russell, Garden Terrace; John McKie, Castle Street; Arthur Tallis, Balfour Street; John Sinclair, Bruce Street, and John Neil from The Green, all serving with the Argylls.

I continued on down to Mr & Mrs Rorrison's sweetie shop on the corner where Castle Street joins Main Street and the Cattle Market. Directly opposite is Jean Forsyth's general store where my dad gets his carbide for his pit lamp. As I stood on the corner, I caught sight of several lads from The Green making their way up the Cattle market. They had just come from the swing-park at the bottom and were making their way home. After a brief exchange, they mentioned that my brother John was still down there with some others from our Terrace.

I headed straight down the steep incline of the Cattle Market and crossed the main Alloa road. As soon as I entered the Park, I spotted a few familiar faces, but no sign of my brother and his pals.

Emma Mitchell, Morag Marshall and Elizabeth Flynn; girls from our Terrace, and all around my age, were playing on the old wooden roundabout. I walked up and asked them if they had seen my brother John. Emma said that John and the others headed off in the direction of The Pottery (the old Pottery was located beside the banks of the Black Devon River, near the spot where the Mary Bridge crosses it). She said that she heard them talking about some sort of event happening in the middle of the Back Wood.

What she was referring to was a clandestine gambling school that a few of the local men attended each Sunday. The event was called, *The Tossing School*. Two pennies were tossed up into the air and people betted on how they would land: two heads, two tails, odd or even. The activity was also illegal, and now and then, the police would make an attempt to put a stop to the practice—they were never successful.

I made my way out of the park, crossed the railway bridge near Harrower's shop on the corner and set off down the main road past the public school and on towards The Pottery. After passing The Tower Hotel on the edge of town, I approached the entrance to the Back Wood just a short distance down on the left near the bend in the road.

I took a few steps in through the trees and called out after them. There was no reply. This was my first visit to the woods, and standing there just a few yards in under the woodland canopy, I had this strange feeling. It was like stepping into another time zone. The pines were tall and quite dense. The wide pathway cutting through the woodland was at one time a single line railway track leading towards the Craigrie Pit. It had branched off just before the main Kincardine line crossed the Black Devon River.

I walked slowly along the now spongy path covered in thick dead pine needles. I kept calling out, but still no reply. The only sound drifting through the trees was the hoot of woodpigeons, and I imagined I heard something scurrying about in the undergrowth. I looked back in the direction of the entrance. I had had enough. I turned and walked back towards the sunlight.

As I stood at the edge of the Back Wood, contemplating what to do next, I turned and walked down the main road to where the Mary Bridge crosses the Black Devon River. I stood on the bridge gazing down at the river winding its way through the trees, and lapsed into my favourite daydream about rafts and Red Indian canoes, wondering what it was like just passed the first bend. Then suddenly a car crossing the bridge startled me.

As I stood watching the car drive up passed the local cemetery and disappear around the corner in the direction of Alloa, I suddenly realised, the old Victorian bridge I mentioned earlier is just around that corner; only a few hundred yards further on. A spark of excitement stirred in me, and I thought, maybe I could just walk to as far as the corner … to the cemetery gate … just to see if I can at least see the bridge from there.

I walked with a new purpose up the small brae towards the cemetery. Several army vehicles trundled passed on their way to the drill hall in North Street, and when I was about half way towards the cemetery, the local bus appeared from around the corner. It headed down the brae, over the Mary Bridge and on through town.

Eventually, I reached the cemetery gate and crossed over the Helensfield road. I stood directly opposite a gatehouse on the corner: the east entrance to Alloa House. There in the distance, I could now make out the familiar shape of my objective. It seemed so far away; and yet the nagging feeling that I had come so far just to turn around and head home seemed such a wasted opportunity.

Without thinking, I took a few steps forward, and another few, and then just after passing a small maintenance hut by the side of the railway track, I started feeling quite encouraged. My pace increased as the objective ahead seemed only minutes away. Then suddenly, from behind, I heard a cry. I turned round and saw a couple of older lassies on bicycles. They were calling my name. As they got closer, I recognised them. It was the Cleghorn sisters; our next-door neighbour's lassies. As I stood there watching them approach, it suddenly dawned on me. Their mission was to take me back with them. They were wholly intent on scuttling my objective.

I turned towards the bridge. It was just forty or fifty yards ahead. This chance would never come again. I ran as fast as my young legs could carry me. I just wanted to climb those steps and reach the top; but it was not to be. A bicycle whizzed past and blocked my path. Words like: *"Your mother has been worried sick!"* drowned out my pleas to complete my mission.

Apparently, the girls in the swing park met up with them and told them where I was heading. When they cycled down near the Pottery, they met up with some friends who got off the local bus—my whereabouts were revealed. I was taken straight home without any more nonsense. The desire to make another attempt never returned … it was, I suppose, a bridge too far.

*The bridge too far…*

# Chapter 3
# The Summer Break

The warm sunny days during the school holidays were often spent bathing (and sometimes without swimming trunks) down at the *Dookin Hole;* our favourite swimming spot at the bottom of the Riccarton where the Goudnie Burn meets the Black Devon. The deepest bit was about three feet, safe enough for wading and splashing about.

Some of the older lads would climb the tree near the bank and do what they called, a *Depth Charge* (an explosive charge used by the Royal Navy to sink submarines). They would leap off the tree into the river holding their knees tight under their chins, creating as close as possible the plume shape rush of water as *the Charge* exploded under the sea.

During those early years, I stayed close to the riverbank; I still hadn't mastered the technique of actually swimming, but it was great fun just pretending by bellying along the warm muddy banks.

Further down at the shallower end near the spot where the Goudnie enters the river, some tried their hand at catching small fish in empty jam jars. The species of fish caught determined one's level of skill; for example, young beginners usually managed to trap the smallest ones called *Baggie Minnows*. They swam about in bunches and were quite easy to herd into the open jar, while other species, like *Katie Bairdies*, or the elusive *Red Stickleback,* took a great deal more know-how and patience.

*Our favourite swimming spot: the Dookin Hole…*

Further up the river, grown-ups caught trout using nothing but their bare hands. The technique was called *guddlin.* The idea was to lean over the bank or wade out among the submerged rocks, patiently wait until you spotted the body and tail of a trout under a rock, and then gently tickle its belly. I suppose you then just grabbed it. However, I'm sure there's more to it than that; a level of skill I was never able to achieve.

During a break, as we stood on the riverbank with our towels wrapped around our shoulders, someone suggested we should try further up the river. Apparently, there is a great spot in the Ladywood called *The Dead Man's Hole*, and another place a short distance further on at the Linn Mill falls.

As soon as we changed back into our clothes, we set off along the path, climbed the embankment where the bridge crosses the river and took the road that forked off towards the Cherryton Brickworks. After passing an old disused quarry a hundred yards or so up on our right, the lad leading the way turned and indicated that we should now enter the woodland.

After treading through a bit of undergrowth, he soon found the narrow footpath, almost hidden under the lush green woodland plants. As we made our way along it, I noticed the bank immediately on our left getting a lot steeper, and the sound of the river below gradually increasing as it flowed through a small section of rapids. I began to get a wee bit nervous at the thought of slipping down it. At the same time, I was fascinated with the jungle like setting: the tall trees, wild flowers, shrubs of all sorts, and through it all, the sounds of hooting woodpigeons, warbling birds, and rushing water.

Then suddenly, appearing through the trees was this enormous railway viaduct with great arches spanning the river below. It was the main Alloa/Dunfermline railway line. I remembered having seen this bridge before, but I don't recall ever having come this particular way.

The pathway eventually descended quite steeply towards the river's edge, but just before it did, one of our party pointed to a strange fenced off spot to our right and warned us never to venture into it. It was an old mine airshaft, and I must say, the fence around it was in a very poor state. It wouldn't be the first time that curiosity got the better of some unfortunate lad. As I moved passed it, I felt a cold shiver all down me. It was like passing the entrance to something evil.

We started making our way down the path, holding onto some of the tough vegetation to steady our descent. At this point, the sounds of the rapids faded and the river now flowed at a gentle pace. We stood for several minutes under the enormous arches of the viaduct and listened to our voices echoing all around us. Just then, a short distance along the riverbank, we heard voices. It was a couple of young men from our town. They had just finished fishing and were sorting out their catch. When we asked how well they did, one of them opened up a bunch of cut grass they used as a wrapper to keep the fish fresh and displayed several reasonable sized trout.

One of our lads asked if they were caught by hand; meaning, were they guddled. They said: 'Of course!' This led on to the various methods and techniques, and it was then that I became aware of the different types of trout. This particular catch was a species of trout common to this region. They called them *salmon trout*. The colourful globular markings on their skins were quite remarkable.

Normally I hated fish because of the bones; however, this particular species was very tasty. On one occasion, my Dad happened to bring home two or three that were given to him by some angling friend of his. They were delicious, not quite as strong as salmon (I had only experienced the tin variety) and the bones were soft enough to eat. We left the two men and headed further along the river.

Just ahead of us, I saw a familiar looking structure; a narrow concrete footbridge spanning the river. As soon as we climbed up onto the adjoining footpath, I realised where we were. This was where Ma and Dad had taken us on an Easter picnic a year or so before. Our picnic spot lay just across the footbridge and a short distance along the left bank of the river. It was a small clearing among the trees with a beautiful patch of green grass like a well-tended lawn. I remember the McCards from Balfour Street were already there with their Billycans, and they even had a large ex-army cooking pot suspended over a small campfire boiling up some spuds. They seemed to have it all properly thought out, with their picnic rug, their plates, forks and knives, and even a bottle of HP Sauce.

Our gang of would-be swimmers continued along the left bank of the river until we reached a bend where the going ahead got too difficult. At this spot, we had to make our way across to the opposite bank. Fortunately, this section of the river was quite shallow and rocky, making the crossing reasonably straightforward. As soon as we crossed over, we moved on. The pathway ahead rose quite steeply and gradually we lost sight of the river as we made our way up the side of a small gorge. The noise of rushing water seemed to ease a little, and then just a few yards ahead, the lads in front paused. They were pointing down at something through the trees. I squeezed my way through towards the edge of the embankment and suddenly, there it was, just below us … the *Dead Man's Hole.*

The sight of it sent goose bumps right through me; the whole atmosphere rang alarm bells. It was as if people had shaped it; as if a team of miners attempted to dig out a great wide shaft and abandoned it only to be filled up by the river; and as clear as it was, I could not see the bottom.

One of the lads, renowned for his sense of melodrama, said in slow drawn out tones: *"No one has yet been able to find-out the depth of it."* I just stood there holding onto a tree trunk while staring down at the still water as if something evil lurked just below the surface.

We moved on a bit further and found a narrow track that gave access to the river below. At this point, the river rushed wildly through a narrow gorge, cascaded over large boulders and rock pools before gently flowing into the stillness of the *Dead Man's Hole.*

*The falls at Linn Mill…*

Some of the older lads began stripping off, getting themselves ready to take the plunge. As the more adventurous swam through the narrow gorge and into the hole, the sound of their yells and shouts bounced off the steep rocky banks creating an eerie echoic effect. I sat on the rocks, my feet dangling in the cold bubbling water and looked around the spot we had chosen to play in. A hundred yards or so up stream, I could see the road bridge that crossed the river at Linn Mill. From this angle, its single stone arch looked enormous.

One of my pals said there was another great swimming spot just on the other side of the bridge, situated beside the remains of an old watermill. As he described the place, I remembered, I had been there before during that Easter picnic with my parents. After we finished our picnic, Ma and Dad had taken us for a stroll through the trees. We walked up a wide track towards the Clackmannan/Forest Mill road, stepped over the large wooden stile and strolled down the short distance towards Linn Mill.

The actual village of Linn Mill is really just a hamlet of around half a dozen terraced cottages just across the bridge. At the rear of the cottages, the ground slopes down towards the old watermill situated beside the riverbank. It was first used in the late sixteenth century as a grain mill and later finished up a sawmill.

On the left, just before crossing the bridge, a narrow dirt road wide enough for a horse and cart descends steeply and crosses the river over another small stone bridge towards the mill.

Standing at the edge of the mill and looking out at the waterfalls was an exciting moment, and seeing that great big waterwheel at the side of the shed with the manmade channel running along the side of it, was quite spectacular. I had never come across a place quite like it before, but that was not all. This spot had its own *Wishing-Well.* It was actually my Dad who gave it the name. He came across it as we made our way back up the steep track to the road.

Across the small stone bridge and about halfway up on the right, he noticed a narrow opening with stone steps leading down to the edge of the river. He decided to investigate. A few steps down, he found a small cave that looked like a sort of mysterious grotto. In it sat a large baked piggy-clay trough. It was square shaped and about three feet high. The rocky sides of the tiny cave constantly dripped with water that over time filled the trough. The water was as clear as crystal, cold and quite delicious. It had just a slight flavour of ferns and moss. Some locals named this place, *The Cold Water Rock,* but Dad's *Wishing-Well* version remained with us for many years.

Those summer days spent playing along the Black Devon River were great fun, and one day soon, I would eventually learn to swim. However, in the meantime, I was just as content wading and splashing about in the shallows.

The way home was a pleasant stroll through the wood and across farmer Norvall's fields. Some of us got a bit burnt with too much exposure to the sun causing all sorts of stinging discomfort. The worst cases were the peeling skin that left us itching for days. But, some paraded their pink skins with pride and called it suntan. A day or so later it all vanished, back to our true colour … white.

## Visiting the Relatives

For some of us, the summer break often included a trip to the seaside, or spending some time with the relatives. As both my parents were originally from the Lothians, it meant that their annual holiday gave them the opportunity to pay the rest of the family an extended visit. Dad's parents and most of his siblings lived in Prestonpans, East Lothian; and Ma's side of the family were mainly in and around Musselburgh, Mid Lothian.

When the day arrived, we all rose reasonably early, got ourselves spruced up, and headed off to catch the bus. The sight of us all walking together down the road, dressed in our Sunday best, gave the occasion an air of excitement and adventure.

We had to make three bus changes: the first bus took us to Falkirk, where we boarded another, taking us all the way to St Andrew's Square, Edinburgh, and from there, the final leg of the journey to our destination: Prestonpans.

Our first port of call was Granny and Granddad's place in Summerlea Street at Cuthill. Their home was in a typical row of two story miners dwellings built around the end of the Victorian era. The road surface running beside it was merely compressed earth edged with stone guttering, and across the road opposite, stood the washhouses.

Granny and Granddad lived in the ground floor apartment. Their front door led directly into the kitchen and scullery. A bathroom with toilet was just to the right of that; and immediately to the left, a door gave access to the living area.

The first thing that confronted you as you entered the sitting room was the fireplace; it was enormous, an old Victorian cast iron type with facilities to accommodate a pot or kettle. The pots would be placed on gridiron rests mounted at the sides of the grate, and swung in over the flames. Above the high mantelpiece, and protruding from the wall, was the gas mantle; the only source of evening light.

The other impressive item in the room stood against the adjacent wall. It was a huge windpipe organ. It stood about six or seven feet high and had decorative shelves of various sizes. A lid opened up displaying rows of ivory and ebony keys, and running above them, rows of push-pull knobs that adjusted the pitch or tone. Perhaps, due to the introduction of radio, the instrument was very rarely used. The room also had a very large cavity bed that accommodated all us youngsters, including Ma. I still have fond memories of us all lying snugly in that big bed with the curtain drawn and listening to the grown-ups chatting around the fireside; in particular, the powerful resonant tone of Granddad's voice as he sat in his armchair puffing away on his white clay pipe; and every now and then, there would be a sharp explosive hiss from the hot coals as Granddad let go with a well-directed spit. The men talked mainly about work related issues, while the women chatted on the side-line about family and friends. With the drone of adult voices in our ears, and the gentle hiss of the gas light on the wall above the fireplace, we soon drifted off to sleep.

The following morning we had a couple of visitors. Uncle Hughie and Aunty Martha's two daughters, Margaret and Catharine. Uncle Hughie also had two sons, Bobby and Jim; however, they were quite a few years older than we were. Dad's other siblings were his youngest brother Bobby and his two sisters Mary and Jeannie.

Margaret and Catherine had brought along their dog Blackie, a black shaggy haired mongrel with a cheerful disposition. It was the sister to Granny and Granddad's dog, Lady; pronounced in the East Lothian dialect … *Leddie*.

The noise of excited cousins and dogs running amok in the living room stirred us into action. We dressed as quickly as we could, and after a quick slosh under the scullery tap, we were off out to play. The first place we headed for was the seafront.

The seafront at Prestonpans is not your typical holiday seaside resort: pebbles, seashells, and rocky outcrops. Not a trace of sand anywhere, except a couple of miles further down the coast at Port Seaton. However, as we lived quite a distance from the nearest seaside, anywhere by the sea was always a great treat.

The two dogs hit the beach like a couple of excited kids, while we ran about along the shoreline enjoying the seaside atmosphere, the smell of the salty air, and the sound of the waves crashing on the shingle.

Further up the beach, we could see some people with hand buckets collecting something lying about the shore. When I asked Margaret what they were doing, she told me they were picking up small lumps of coal. Apparently, they came from seams located just under the surface and washed up by the surf. Some of the local kids could even earn themselves an extra bob or two selling the coal around the doors.

While standing about on the edge of the shore looking out across the water, I heard through the noise of the crashing surf, the sound of my dad's voice. I turned and looked up to see both my parents waving at us over the sea wall.

We made our way up the stone steps towards them. My mother told us that she and my younger brother Andrew were heading off to visit our other Grandparents in Musselburgh, and that she would most likely be spending a few nights there. She wanted to know if we were happy to remain here in Prestonpans with Dad.

To be perfectly honest, both John and I were more than happy to stay where we were. I much preferred to be here in *The Pans* than at Grandma Stanton's house in Musselburgh. She was a tough disciplinarian, a no nonsense old matriarch from good Irish stoke. Her home was immaculate, filled to capacity with beautiful old style furniture: writing bureau, piano, grandmother-clock, and richly decorated cabinets all polished to perfection. Laying so much as a grubby toffee laden finger on them would herald the wrath from somewhere above, like the back of Grandma's hand. We had to sit there and behave. It seemed to me that she regarded bairns as just a whole barrel of trouble, and yet she had six of her own; three boys and three girls … how on earth did she manage.

Of course now, I fully appreciate, as people get older, they value different things, like *peace and quiet,* and nice things around them without the risk of active bairns running about breaking the trinkets.

Grandpa Stanton was just the opposite. He was a quiet man, softly spoken, a little bit on the rotund side, which added something to his character, and always well dressed with his gold watch and chain looped about his waistcoat. He enjoyed sitting in his armchair smoking his pipe and listening to the races on the wireless.

In comparison, my Dad's parents were the opposite. Granny Wood was this meek little old woman who pottered about the house doing her chores; while Granddad was a giant of a man; an ex-Regimental Sergeant Major, fought with General Allenby in the Middle East during WW1. He was over six feet in height and had a resonant voice that could be heard from one end of town to the other.

As we watched Ma and Andrew board the SMT coach bound for Musselburgh, Dad just happened to notice a couple of his old pals make their way into the Gothenburg; a popular local public house a few doors down from the bus stop. He wasted no time in telling us of his immediate intentions. He put his hand into his pocket, pulled out some change and handed John a half-crown piece, telling him to buy some chips for all of us at Aunty Nellie's … Aunty Nellie was not a relative. The name is a misnomer; one of my many mispronunciations when confronting the unfamiliar, especially exotic names from foreign parts. The correct name is Antonelli, an Italian proprietor of the local fish and chip restaurant.

Making our way towards the chip shop, we saw Uncle Bobby heading for the Gothenburg. He stopped to talk to Margaret and said that we should call on Alex and Dan. Uncle Bobby has a family of four sons and one daughter. The oldest was Bert, about the same age as my brother John, maybe a little older; then Alex and Dan, around my age. As for the youngest ones, Freddy and Fay, I would get to know them much later on.

After picking up our bag of chips, we made our way up Red Burn Road towards their house. Aunty Annie answered the door and let us in. She took us all through the house towards the back garden.

There in the garden, we found Cousin Bert in the process of attaching a set of wheels to a piece of wood using a few rusty old nails hammered in with the blunt end of an axe. Dan and Alex were happily assisting him. When asked what they were doing, Alex told us that they were making a trolley. They had come across this old pram down at the dump and removed the set of wheels from it.

I took particular notice of how they made this interesting toy. I fancied I could make one for myself; all I needed were the materials and a little instruction.

*The Trawley...*

There were two types of self-made toys commonly built by the lads a few years ago. Some made the two-wheel version called, *the barrow*. All you needed was a set of wheels, a wooden box big enough for a youngster to sit in, and two lengths of timber nailed to the sides of the box to act as handles. One person would pretend to be the horse and pull the barrow along with the handles, or just simply push it along. The other type, *the trolley*, was in my opinion, the more interesting of the two. However, it needed two sets of wheels, sometimes found in the rubbish tips on old discarded prams; you had to be lucky, it was always a question of being in the right place at the right time.

As Bert and Alex put the final touches to their creation, they were then eager to try it out. Bert had the first go while we all took it in turn pushing from behind. Everything seemed to operate pretty well. It all looked a great deal of fun, and I felt at that moment a bit impatient to get back home and build my own.

After a while, we made our way back to Granny's place. As soon as we entered the living room, we met another couple of cousins, Jean and Mary. They were Uncle Jock and Aunty Jeannie's lassies. They lived in Tranent, a town just a mile or so to the south east of the Pans. Uncle Jock was keen to see my Dad and as soon as Margaret informed him of his precise location, both he and Granddad promptly stirred themselves into action and headed off in the direction of the Gothenburg.

Shortly after, Catherine and Margaret made their way back up the road to their parents place at the top of Summerlea. Then a short time later, while John and I were out the front of Granny's place playing, we saw the figure of Uncle Hughie making his way across the vacant lots towards, apparently, that very popular pub: the Gothenburg.

Evenings spent with the cousins were very enjoyable. I particularly liked the stories told to us around the fireside. I voted Uncle Hughie the best storyteller of the family, not just because of the way he told them, it was the facial expressions, that dramatic look on the face, and his bushy eyebrows adding to the effect. There we would be, sitting around the fireside with just the glow from the coals and gas mantle.

*Ghost stories around the fireside…*

My favourite story, and the one that scared me the most, was the one where this particular fellow took shelter from a downpour in an old empty house. He came across a perfectly good bed sheet and a large marrowbone. He took the articles home and made soup with the bone, and placed the sheet on his bed.

Shortly after that, he had a visitor, a dark slow moving ghoul. Its breathing was heavy and deep, and it began speaking in a low trembling voice, saying: *"... I want my sheet and my marrowbone."* It kept repeating the same sentence over and over, and getting closer and closer. Even though we heard the story several times before, we were all on edge. The shock came, after the ghoul closed in on his victim with a sudden increase in volume on the last word: *"... I want my sheet and my marrow-BONE!"* The effect was always the same with us all ending up thrown back in our chairs.

Then later, just before bed, Aunty Martha would bring in a plate of freshly cooked melted cheese on toast.

How different things were back then, the way evenings were spent before the introduction of television. There were conversations around the fireside, storytelling, playing games or musical instruments, or just sitting quietly reading a novel. I suppose with every change comes a degree of progress, but it seems there is always a price to pay.

All our other activities in the Pans consisted of running about the cousin's favourite play sights, sneaking into the golf course looking for lost golf balls, or playing along the shoreline. Occasionally, Dad would feel the need for a bit of a walk and I would be asked to join him. John, on the other hand preferred to remain playing with the older cousins.

Dad liked his walks, and I enjoyed his company. We would visit such places as the old ruins of Falside Castle, or along the coast, sometimes taking the short bus trip to Port Seton.

The beach at Port Seton was as I imagined a beach should be; all beautiful pristine golden sand stretching for several miles along the coast towards Aberlady Point. Curious looking great concrete blocks, measuring around four or five feet high, ran along the edge of the coastline. Dad explained that their purpose was to prevent German tanks landing on that part of the coast. Whatever they were, many people found them very handy, using them as windbreaks when picnicking beside the beach.

While Dad sat down on a convenient rock, taking a short break to enjoy one of his extra strong Cogent cigarettes (a brand produced by the Scottish Co-operative Wholesale Society), I ran about over the sand dunes. There seemed to be quite a number of people on the beach that day. Some relaxing on their large towels, and a few even had deckchairs; all lounging about, and enjoying the seaside ambiance. Some of the men sat with their trouser legs rolled up just below the knee, and a few had hankies on their head with knots tied on each corner—this was to protect their baldheads from sunburn.

As for the kids, they each had their *bucket and spade*, and busied themselves with the popular seaside activity of sand castle building. A few of the castles were really quite cleverly constructed with moats all the way round the perimeter, compacted sand forming the bridges, and little paper flags stuck on the turrets. The congeniality of the scene was very pleasant.

I made my way down to the edge of the water and played that game of trying to race the tide back up the beach without getting my feet wet. The screaming of gulls and the swishing of the surf added to, what was for me, a very enjoyable day.

After a while, I looked back towards the spot where Dad was resting and noticed he had company. It was a man about the same age as him and they appeared to be engaged in light-hearted conversation. I headed back towards them. As I approached, Dad turned and introduced me to his companion.

He was an old pal from the time before our family moved to Clackmannan. They continued talking about the old days; most of the people they mentioned were totally unknown to me. I sat down on the sand and pottered about, half-listening. As they reminisced about the old times, one particular story caught my attention. It was an amusing anecdote that could have had fatal consequences.

During the war, dad worked as a coalminer, a reserved occupation (shortly after war was declared, both he and Granddad joined the Home Guard). One day, while working down the pit, he met with an accident. The roof caved in and completely buried him. Some of the rescuers were actually stepping on top of him not knowing he lay just beneath the rubble. He managed to make a sound of sorts, letting them know that he was just below their feet. They soon dug him out, and shortly after he left hospital, he spent the next few weeks on crutches.

Then, one particular day, a week or so after the accident, he and a few of his pals went for a walk along the shore at Prestonpans. They walked slowly in respect of Dad's injury; he also had a tough time negotiating the pebbly beach with his crutches. Then one of the lads suddenly spotted an aerial dogfight over the water. Fighter planes were attacking some German bombers.

As Dad and his pals stood on the beach watching the drama unfold, one of the bombers began trailing smoke. It banked to the left and descended in the direction of our beachfront spectators. Directly behind it and in hot pursuit came an RAF fighter, its guns blazing. The fountain-like effects of bullets splashing along the edge of the water and up the beach caused Dad's companions to scattered in all directions leaving him struggling franticly across the loose pebbles with his crutches.

Behind him, the deafening roar of the bomber's engines got closer as if about to land on top of him. He dropped face down onto the beach and hoped for the best. The beach pebbles rattled and vibrated all around him as the aircraft passed over, and directly behind it, the fighter. Bullets strafed along each side of him and the roar of the fighter's engine screamed overhead.

Seconds later, the noise of guns and aircraft engines faded over the horizon, and but for the sound of the lapping surf, there was silence … it was over.

The bomber apparently crashed several miles further on. Dad's pals raced back down the beach and helped him up, all agreeing unanimously that what was needed at that moment in time was a couple of calming beverages, and without further debate, they headed off in the direction of the Gothenburg.

The time had come for us all to return to Clackmannan. Dad, John and I were to take the bus into Musselburgh to pick up Ma and Andrew at our other Grandparents place in Stoneybank Gardens. We had spent the last day visiting Uncle Jock and Aunty Jeannie in Tranent. Their first three kids were, Bobby, Jim and Cathy, who were a lot older than both John and I were, so we didn't have much to do with them as far as infant pursuits were concerned. Jean and Mary were about our age; however, they appeared more reserved, like a couple of normal young lassies. I much preferred the mischievous adventures with Dan and Alex.

Granny accompanied us down to the bus stop just outside the Gothenburg. From inside the bus, I sat waving to her as we moved off. She looked very old world, a product of the Victorian age with her shawl wrapped around her shoulders. As we turned the first corner past the Co-op buildings and the primary school at Cuthill, I took one last look out to sea and thought, how lucky my cousins were to live in an area so close to a beach … albeit a pebbly one.

On arriving in Musselburgh, we took another bus up the west side of the Esk River towards Stoneybank Gardens. Gran and Grandpa Stanton's house was a semi-detached block containing four separate residences. The exterior walls were pebble dashed with grey coloured stones. They also had front and rear gardens. Built sometime before the war, they were a lot smarter looking than our other grandparents place in Summerlea.

The house also has a special significance for me … I was born in it. My mother showed me the room where the event took place. I was born at four o'clock on the morning of 1 April 1943—April-Fools Day.

Apparently, there was an air raid in progress. Ma said she could hear the spent rounds from the anti-aircraft guns rattling off the tiled roof. An explosion from a large bomb called a *landmine* was heard somewhere to the west. I don't know where Dad was. I think I heard my Ma say he was out partying somewhere.

Before departing on the last leg of our journey home, Ma was busy in the kitchen filling her bag with Grandma's homemade cakes. The family used to be bakers and before they moved into their present house, they had a small shop near the centre of town; Dam Brae, I heard my mother call the place. Grandma turned out to be a gifted baker. Her cakes and pastries were truly delicious: Dundee cakes, black bun, cherry cakes, jam tarts, snowballs, all baked to perfection. My mother would try to copy her methods; however, although her cakes and tarts were delicious, they didn't have that extra special touch of Grandma's. I think Ma's philosophy was, near enough was good enough.

Soon we were all ready to make our way down to the bus stop. Grandma and Ma walked arm in arm while Dad strode ahead with Grandpa. The bus soon came and we were off to catch the connection at Saint Andrew's Square in Edinburgh. This was always the boring part of the journey, the hanging about for the next bus to take us on to our next connection at Falkirk. By the time we arrived home, we were all exhausted.

# Chapter 4
# Autumn Approach

The wheat crops in the surrounding fields had now grown to full height and their colour already changing to harvest gold. At this stage, we would run through the high stalks, treading pathways like trails through a maze, and creating wee hideaways.

The local policeman was kept busy during these holiday periods, pursuing and apprehending mischievous kids. Old PC Meldrum, the policeman who found me that day at the Tulligarth Pit, and who took me home in handcuffs, had retired. His replacement was this very tall fine figure of a man with the facial expression appropriate to his station, as guardian of the local property—and the peace. We knew him as PC Kettles. He was a family man with three tall children; the oldest was a girl. As she was quite a few years older than I was, I never got to know her. His two sons, Victor and Ross were more our age. I was to meet Ross later in the classroom.

*Enter PC Kettles…*

Although PC Kettles was big in stature and easy to spot, he still had that knack of catching us unaware. More often than not, we would be lined-up in front of him, his large bicycle with its double crossbar propped behind him, and his notebook and pencil at the ready, meticulously filling in all our names and addresses.

I got to wondering after a while why he went through the same process of taking all our names and addresses; he knew us all by sight anyway, and precisely where we lived. There may have been a bit of psychology about the whole process when I think back on it. It gave the incidents, no matter how trivial, an air of grave consequence—of being brought to book!

Of course, if the misbehaviour was really serious, it would then take the form of an official visit to confront our parents. The humiliation of it would incite dire consequences, like Dad's leather belt across our backsides.

Mischievous activities never set out to be anything other than creative playing; but of course, most infants have no concept of the cost to the victim. Not just the few missing apples or pears from their trees, but the flattened fence, the trampled flowerbeds, and the broken branches left behind during these infuriatingly naughty deeds. However, having said all that, most of the time our activities were just innocent fun … in my opinion.

My playmates were mainly from the Terrace, and The Green. The actual number of kids in The Green seemed countless; however, in the Terrace, I recall there were about eighteen of us; half of those were lassies.

Our favourite playing areas were the adjacent fields and woodlands. A large overgrown two-acre piece of ground belonging to auld Haerie Ferguson, had a well-worn footpath leading down to what was once a sports area (now completely populated with houses). The field that once ran from the top of the Look-Aboot-Ye-Brae along the edge of the small woodland was in fact Chapelhill Park, once the home of the local soccer team. The Alloa Athletic football team played their first Club League match against the home team there on the 27th August 1921. Alloa won, beating Clackmannan by 2 goals to 1.

*The old Curling Pond and Pavilion…*

Situated next to the old football park, and in line with the high stonewall that edged the woodland, was the sight of the old Curling-Pond. Just before the war, the area belonged to the Clackmannan & Kennet Curling Club, and the proprietor was James Adams of Meadowend Farm. Several tall Scotch-Pine trees stood at the east end of it, and a red brick pavilion was located at the west end, built partway into the woodland. A small opening at the side led into the woods. When the sight was abandoned after the war, some locals began slowly looting the place, using the materials for small personal building projects: a shed, a hen house, or pigeon loft.

A year before, the older lassies from The Green held an impromptu concert in the old pavilion just before the looters got their hands on it. My mother and a few of the women from The Green and the Terrace were invited to the grand opening. We sat around in a semi-circle on makeshift benches and watched the performances. There was singing and dancing, and things like simple magic tricks. Everything appeared well organised and the whole spectacle was quite impressive.

However, the plaster coverings on the ceiling had been removed, leaving the rafter beams exposed, and during the show, some mischievous lads climbed up onto the beams. They began disrupting the performances by dropping things on the lassies' heads and generally making a damned nuisance of themselves. Every now and then, the mothers in the audience would let out with a few heated remarks, like: *"Ya wee buggers! If I get my hands on you, I'll skelp your arses!"*

But this just encouraged the wee buggers. However, the lassies pressed on to the final curtain without too much disruption.

Another favourite playing spot was Geordie Gray's yard. His property ran from Balfour Street all the way down to the old curling ponds. He kept a number of old wrecked cars and some ex-army vehicles down at the end of his property. Apparently, Geordie didn't mind the local kids playing among the old wrecks, as long as they didn't venture up near his house or the workshop. To all members of *The Green Gang*, this was their territory; interlopers were not allowed. The Zetland Street boys of course hotly disputed this, and many a pitch battle was fought on the road leading up to our territory. Our weapons were catapults, arrows, and spears. The neighbours' bucket-lids were used as shields.

When I look back on those days, I'm always amazed that there were no serious injuries during the confrontations. Showers of stone projectiles rained down on both sides. The spears and arrows were reasonably harmless, but the catapults sometimes caused a bit of concern. The occasional outburst of pain followed by tears was inevitable.

As a mere infant amidst all this, my contribution to the war effort was next to futile. Still, the numbers counted and serious injuries were rare. Perhaps a degree of common sense prevailed on both sides; after all, they were also our schoolmates. However, I do recollect one serious incident where a young lad lost the tip of his pinkie finger. It did not happen in the heat of battle, nor was he a victim of enemy fire; perhaps it could've been put down to an unfortunate incident of *Friendly Fire*.

It occurred when a few of the lads from Zetland Street were playing down at the Curling-Pond. Their leader, Tucker Glen, decided to introduce a new gang initiation ceremony. He had with him a small hand axe, and each member was to place their hand on the trunk of one of the pine trees. Tucker would then chop as close to their fingers as possible to see who was the bravest. The first to volunteer was young George Solomon, my classmate. He bravely put his hand on the trunk and Tucker promptly chopped off the end of his pinkie. That incident was the most serious I can recall.

As for the lassies, they were not in the least bit interested in most of our activities. They seemed perfectly happy with their skipping ropes, or playing in their back gardens with their dolls and tea sets. Another very popular girl's game at that time was drawing large squares on the streets with white chalk and playing hopscotch, or *beds* as they called it. Either their peevers (shuttles) were an empty shoe polish tin, or ideally a glazed tile from Alex Sime's building supplies down at the Riccarton. They appeared a very passive lot; which brings me to, what I thought, a very uncharacteristic incident.

It happened several years later during yet another confrontation with the Zetland Street boys. The combat zone was the stretch of road between Zetland Street and The Green (now called South Pilmuir Road). It raged on for some time, and on this particular occasion we were a bit outnumbered, gradually pulling back bit-by-bit. It seemed all they had to do was suddenly charge and that would be that. Then, at the corner of my eye, I saw Cathy Cleghorn, our next-door neighbour's oldest daughter, accompanied by a couple of younger lassies. They cautiously tried to make their way past the melee and down the road towards the Square. Then it happened. One of the Zetland Street boys threw a stick meant for one of us, but as luck would have it, the trajectory went a bit off course and hit Cathy squarely across the shins. She let out a loud cry and moments later, there was silence.

*'Ya wee buggers, jist wait till I get my hands on ye!'*

A few seconds passed as she nursed her injury, then suddenly, she picked up the stick and ran straight towards the Zetland Street boys, crying: 'Ya wee buggers, jist wait till I get my hands on ye!' Panic set in. They turned and fled down the brae and disappeared round the corner back into their own street. We were all jubilant, jumping up and down and chanting: 'We won the war … we won the war!'

# The Gang's Great Festive Plan

While playing with a few pals in Geordie Gray's yard, pretending to drive an old 1928 Hillman that still had its beautiful leather upholstery, minus its doors and wheels, my brothers, John and Andrew, turned up with some of the older lads from The Green. Their mission was to build a shelter or camp (generally built from scrap material like, corrugated iron, and pieces of timber salvaged from demolished houses). In this case, the decision was to manoeuvre a couple of the old car bodies and position them next to each other creating an enlarged two-roomed shelter. Heaps of straw would be collected from the paddocks and fields to cover the floor and block up any draughty gaps. After the project was complete, we piled inside it to see how many could comfortably fit in at the one time. It was perfect.

The last remaining days of our summer holidays were spent down at that camp. Occasionally, a campfire would be arranged and sometimes (when in season) tatties from Wullie McAinsh's field would be placed in the hot ash for baking. We could hardly wait to break open the charred blackened skin and eat the hot contents. Occasionally, some very generous lads would share their precious sweeties; the *Penny Dainty* was the usual treat, an over-sized toffee Caramel that we managed to break into small bits.

While we sat enjoying the roast tatties and sweeties, talking about this and that, one of the lads put forward an idea. He said something like: 'Hi! I've got an idea. How about organising a gang party. We could have ourselves a great feast with roast tatties, and maybe we could raid the local orchards for a few apples or pears.'

Now, there were several orchards in and around the town. Some were a bit difficult to access owing to their location; for example, old Mr Dunlop's garden at the top of Castle Street was surrounded by other properties. So, after a moment of consideration, the decision rested on three possible sites: first, old Ja-Ja's orchard at the top of the Look-Aboot-Ye-Brae; second, the orchard at Garden Terrace with its very high perimeter stonewall; and third, the most daring sight of all: the pear tree at the rear of the Manse.

The only trouble with old Ja-Ja's place was that he was, apparently, in possession of a blunderbuss; an old eighteenth century shotgun, and he wasn't afraid to use it. It was said that he filled the trumpet shaped barrel with tiny pellets that caused a great deal of discomfort; especially when aimed at an intruder's backside. I personally never knew anyone who experienced such a fate; however, we all got the picture.

Then there's the small market garden and orchard at Garden Terrace with its very high perimeter wall. A couple of the older lads did manage to scale the great wall, but apparently, it was a very risky business. This left the Manse. The garden at the rear of the Manse had a well-cared-for pear tree. The pears on the Minister's tree were said to be among the tastiest in the parish.

The decision was made and a plan prepared. The pear tree in the garden at the rear of the Manse was the objective. The whole operation would be conducted like a commando raid. As the boys of my age group were too small to get involved, we were therefore delegated to be lookouts.

A frontal approach was out of the question, as it would mean creeping up the noisy gravel driveway, passing the front entrance with its big windows and down the side of the house into the garden at the rear. The occupants were bound to spot us.

The other alternative was the rear approach. Although the garden at the back of the Manse had a nine-foot stonewall surrounding it, it did have a major advantage. The wall could be approached from the High Street through the Kirk gate, and across the graveyard, giving us plenty of cover. And Anthony, one of the older members of the gang solved the problem of scaling the high wall. He said he got the idea a few weeks ago after seeing a war film about commandos at the Gaumont Picture House in Alloa.

It needed three of the fittest boys. The first lad would place himself with his back to the wall and clasp his hands in front of him. The second would step onto his hands, and then up onto his shoulders and climb to the top of the wall. The third would be lifted up and over the wall. Then when a sufficient amount of pears were picked, they would then be thrown back over the wall to the rest of the gang waiting on the other side. Finally, the lad perched on the wall would haul up the lad in the garden. This was the plan. It needed timing and military precision.

We assembled around the old clock tower at the Mercat Cross, the top end of Main Street. I, along with Adam McNeil from our Terrace, and George McQueen from The Green, were given our instructions. We had to position ourselves beside Nellie Grasso's fish and chip shop at the top of Main Street where we would have a clear view of the police station just a short distance down the way. Another couple were positioned further up the High Street opposite the entrance to the churchyard. If we spotted PC Kettles, we would then wave to the others and so on.

All was going as planned. The main party had moved off in the direction of the churchyard, two boys stopped and took up their positions in the High Street, and we stood waiting outside Neillie Grasso's. The minutes passed by, the clock struck the half. Apart from the half dozen or so housewives gossiping in small groups just outside the Cooperative Store, and the couple at the bus stop waiting for the local bus, the streets were reasonably quiet.

Down the Main Street, Alex the barber appeared from his small premises, and leaving his, *Back in five minutes* sign on the door handle, he headed off down the street, disappearing into the main Cooperative office. The only other people around were two men seated on a bench just outside the Royal Oak Hotel at the corner of Port and Main Street.

We stood at our position discussing the forthcoming feast of fruit and roast tatties. Adam thought he might be able to get hold of a bottle of HP sauce from his mother's pantry. He apparently loved HP sauce on his tatties; I must admit, I was partial to a dollop or two myself. Our imaginations were beginning to race out of control. This was going to be an event to remember.

Meanwhile, in the garden of the Manse, the harvesting was going well. Pears were being picked from the branches and dropped onto the beautifully manicured lawn. When a sufficient amount was plucked from the tree, the lad then jumped down and began throwing them over the wall to be scooped up by the waiting army of lads on the other side.

Unfortunately, the operation developed a hitch. From one of the upstairs windows, a curtain was seen to move, and the window suddenly flung open. The head that appeared in the opening was immediately recognised as that of Dr Crouther Gordon, the Minister. He let out a yell: 'You out there! Stay where you are!' An order that Anthony—the lad in the garden—found difficulty obeying. The lad sitting on top of the wall immediately pulled him up leaving the Reverent Dr calling after them.

Back at the number one position outside Neillie Grasso's cafe, one of the men sitting on the bench outside the Royal Oak called me over. His name was Danny Young from The Green, a collier who works with my Dad at Brucefield. The other man sitting beside him was one of the town characters, Serge Aitkin. Serge was well known around the district for his outlandishly funny stories.

Mr Young gave me a message to take to my dad. I was to tell dad that he'll meet him later in the evening at the Horse Shoe Bar; my Dad's favourite pub. Just then, I heard the approach of the local bus labouring up the Port Street brae. At first, I took no notice until it stopped just behind me, quite a distance from the bus stop. Someone was getting off at the corner. Then suddenly, from the main entrance gate to the Manse, the Minister appeared shouting: 'Stop those boys!'

The bus then moved off to reveal the towering figure of PC Kettles, who, as it happened, had hitched a lift up the Port Street brae on the back step of the double-decker bus. The chaos that unfolded before my eyes caused me to freeze in fright. My two pals scattered. They ran straight down in the direction of the Kirk Wynd.

PC Kettles turned to see the others running down the High Street. Panic set in with boys running in all directions. The sergeant major-like shouts from PC Kettles shattered the tranquil scene around the Town Cross with calls of: 'Hey, you lot! Come back here!' The whole street stood watching as some of the lads scampered down the Main Street, darting up the narrow Vennels and Alleyways, the booty of pears dropping out of their bulging jumpers and rolling all over the road.

It was then I felt someone grabbing me from behind. Mr Young picked me up and with great haste guided me through the two swing doors of the Royal Oak bar. He sat me down at a table near the window, and then looked out making sure no one had noticed. After a moment, he turned and said, 'I think you better stay here a minute till everything cools down.' He then crossed over to the bar and returned with a half pint of lemonade and a packet of Smith's Crisps. I sat there in the corner listening to reminiscences of a similar kind from several of the patrons standing around the bar.

After a good twenty minutes or so, Mr Young went outside to survey the situation. He returned moments later and said, 'I think it's safe for you to go now.'

I ventured out, thanking him for the crisps and lemonade. He added that it might not be a good idea to go down the Main Street and advised heading down Port Street.

I stood outside the door of the Royal Oak, cautiously looking around. I was about to head off when I noticed several pears lying across the other side of the road. I ran as quickly as I could, picked them up, and immediately moved off down Port Street, constantly looking back over my shoulder, making sure PC

Kettles was not just round the next corner and appearing as he usually does, as if from nowhere.

I walked on down the brae, passing the Guide Hut at the corner of the road leading down to the Craigrie, and on passed Dr Heatherton's house at Wellmyre. When I reached Ja-Ja's place at the top of the Look-Aboot-Ye-Brae, I made my way into the woodland that ran beside the Curling-Pond. The high wall along the woodland gave me plenty of cover. Then just passed the Curling-Pond I reached the edge of a wheat field. The already formed tracks through the stalks of wheat were an ideal way of approaching the bottom of Castle Street unobserved.

After crawling under the fence, I entered the nearest track and made my way up along the side of the houses at The Green. I then climbed over the fence and stood on the long grassy bank that edged the road leading down to The Square. My home was just around the corner. I was just about to step onto the road and make my way home when I noticed it. Leaning against the wall outside Mr Barr's house was PC Kettles' bicycle. I immediately sprang back up the bank and sank deep into the long grass. Slowly and with much caution, I parted the grass and peered through the tufts. I could just see the bicycle but no sign of PC Kettles, or anyone else. I lay deep in the long glass not daring to move. The minutes passed, the tedium increased and I began to feel just a bit drowsy. The only sounds were the faint buzzing of insects and the occasional gargling noise of turkeys from across the wall in auld Haerie Ferguson's yard.

Lying there, with my chin close to the ground, and waiting on further developments, gradually took its toll. The buzzing and humming sounds of insects were having their effect. I slipped into what seemed another world. There in front of my eyes, small insects were going about their daily chores. A ladybird had just landed halfway up a blade of grass, its wings now being stowed away under its red and black polka-dot coat. I watched it crawl across the strands of grass until eventually it disappeared into the thick tufts. My eyelids were now feeling quite heavy—then suddenly, the sound of voices nudged me back to life. I immediately looked up towards The Green, but saw nothing; then realised the sounds were coming from down the brae. I looked round and saw George and Adam, the two lads who were on guard with me at the town cross. They were walking up from the Square unaware of what lay ahead. I tried to attract their attention and warn them, but they just kept slowly walking up the brae.

Suddenly, the sound of adult voices … P C Kettles had emerged from Mr Barr's house. The two lads on the road immediately stopped when they saw the tall black uniformed figure stepping onto the road ahead. They stood frozen to the spot, completely undecided what to do. Moments later, George turned and spotted me hiding in the long grass. I could see he was about to join me, but it was too late. They were both spotted and immediately summoned by a resonant voice from up the brae.

*'No! Honest Mr Kettles! It wiznie us!'*

I stayed in the long grass and watched helplessly as my two pals moved off to take their medicine. PC Kettles was already taking up the posture of leaning against his bicycle and looking down at my two unfortunate pals.

From where I lay, I could just make out bits of the conversation. I heard Adam's voice saying something like: 'It wiznie me,' and PC Kettles interjecting with: 'Now, now lads, tell the truth!' Then George joining in with: 'No! Honest Mr Kettles! It wiznie us!' The interview finally ended with PC Kettles mounting his bicycle and moving off up Castle Street.

The two lads stood at the corner a moment, and then waved me up to join them. Apparently, they had been seen up at the Cross, but it could not be proved that they were part of this gang of garden raiders. I got the impression that PC Kettles was after bigger fish, not small fry like us.

I headed home feeling a little easier and as I walked through the back door, I saw my mother leaning over the washtub and scrubbing what looked like the weeks washing. I produced three large pears from under my jumper and said, 'I got you a present!' She immediately asked me where I got them. I told her they were just lying about the road, and that they must have fallen off Joe Morrow's fruit cart

# Chapter 5
# Harvest Time

The binders were already at work in the fields, in recent times pulled along by teams of Clydesdale horses. However, the days of the old Clydesdale were ending. Tractors were on the increase around the local farms. The Massey-Ferguson and the little Davie Brown were the usual types.

During harvest time, the familiar figure of Joe the Gerry would be seen perched on the binder behind the tractor. The row of scissor-like teeth cut the stalks of wheat about six inches from the ground, and the great paddles on the binder turning like a Mississippi steamboat, pushed the cut stalks onto a broad canvas conveyer belt, sorted them out into stooks, and tossed them onto the ground.

Some distance behind, a team of farm workers gathered the stooks in bunches and placed them against each other to keep them well aired. They ended up looking like rows of small bivouac tents.

This particular event was one of the highlights of the year, not just for the farming community, but also for some of the local families in the district. It meant the possibility of dining on rabbit pie, or rabbit stew; a welcome change to the post war diet.

Gangs of kids would get together and follow the binders, their cudgels at the ready (a tree branch shaped like a club), waiting to pick off the panic-stricken creatures as they attempted to escape from the ever-diminishing security of the tall stems of wheat. The farmers actually encouraged this activity for it meant a small contribution to the eradication of vermin.

My first experience of such an event was in the late 1940's. On that particular day, my brother John and his pal, Tommy Flynn from No. 8, were out in the back garden preparing their cudgels for the great annual hunt. Both Andrew and I were eager to join them. Others from the Terrace were already making their way down to the field. We soon followed shortly after, heading towards the old Curling-Pond and entering the woodland through the opening at the side of the pavilion. We climbed over the fence surrounding the field and made our way towards the activity. The noise from the other kids already parading behind the binder stirred us into a state of excitement. We couldn't wait to join them.

*Joining the hunt…*

Just minutes after positioning ourselves in a steady walking pace behind the binder, a roar of excitement erupted. A rabbit darted across our path, bobbing and weaving through the crowd of animated kids, cudgels swung franticly over the small creature, its white tail flashing about through the already cut stooks lying about the field. Every now and then, two or three would appear at the same time creating a problem of choice. Inevitably, a few escaped making their way across the field, through the fence and into the thick plantation undergrowth.

John and Tommy were having outstanding success, and Andrew and I were delegated the minders of the catch. As the harvesting progressed, we had to move the dead creatures on to keep up, their warm floppy bodies increasingly difficult to carry.

Eventually, the binder approached the last remaining stalks of wheat. I thought that was that, no point continuing, but I was in for a surprise. The ones too frightened to make a dash for freedom across the open field had moved in towards the middle of the ever-diminishing bit of cover left in the field. Suddenly, faced with no alternative, they darted out in all directions. Moments later, it was all over.

Before Joe and his workmate set about preparing the binder ready for the short trip back to the farm, John asked them for a few lengths of string to tie up their catch. Meanwhile, as all the other participants in the hunt collected theirs, and began making their way back across the field towards town, John and Tommy had other plans.

Halfway along the high ridge on the south side of the field is a circular fenced off area the size of a football pitch. The spot is known locally as *The Roundel*. The interior is a dense over-grown patch of bramble bushes, gooseberry bushes, and long thick matted grass. As soon as the rabbits were tied up in pairs, we made our way up the rise towards a spot at *The Roundel's* perimeter fence.

John and Tommy hopped over the fence and disappeared into the dense interior leaving Andrew and I guarding the rabbits. Occasionally, we heard their cries of pain from being scratched by the thorns. Some minutes later, there was silence. We sat on the grassy bank surrounding the perimeter, the dead rabbits lay at our feet, their big dark eyes already fading to a pitiful milky film. Andrew played with a couple, pretending they were Mr and Mrs Bunny from the animal world of *Brer Rabbit*, moving their heads and legs like marionette puppets.

Moments later, I heard a familiar sound coming from somewhere above. The noise of engines … Rolls Royce engines. There, over on my right and flying in formation was a squadron of Spitfires. Dad mentioned earlier that they were most likely based at the Edinburgh RAF aerodrome.

*Spitfires passing overhead…*

Even though the war had ended two or three years before, there was still quite a fair amount of military activity going on around the local district. A few months before, there was a bit of excitement when the army parked an anti-aircraft gun in the vacant paddock at the corner of The Green and Castle Street. The bigger boys were all over it. I sat on it while someone operated the handle that swung the unit around like a merry-go-round. It was tremendous fun. Then every now and then, we would see the night sky being searched by several very strong searchlights, and even the sound of the air raid siren at the back of the police station in Main Street … I suppose they were just practicing.

Across the field, the last of the hunters were making their way through the woodland and up the footpath towards The Green. Although most of them were quite a distance away, I could still hear some of their voices. Looking back on our childhood days, I must say we did a helluva lot of shouting.

Standing at the end of the footpath on the corner of Castle Street and The Green, was one young lass. She stood calling out to her two brothers playing near Geordie Gray's yard. 'Bobby! Oor Bobby,' she kept calling.

A few seconds later the reply: 'Whaaatt!'

She continued with, 'Ma Maw wants ye!'

'Whaaattt!'

'Maaaw wants ye!' … it's a wonder we didn't all end up with throat problems.

Just to the left and adjoining Geordie Gray's property, I could see old Mr Chalmers in his small allotment feeding his pigeons. Access to his allotment is from Dukestreet, one of the oldest areas in town. Actually, just a few years before, this area was like a separate community and marked on the old map in one word, DUKESTREET. Most of the occupants in the early years were coalminers, as were the people of The Green, and The Square.

One of the shameful chapters in recent Scottish history was the fact that coalminers were actually slaves. Entire families were the property of mine owners until the British Parliament passed a law banning such practices. The closing stage of this system was a gradual process which began in 1775, allowing people to enter this type of employment without holding them to it, and finally allowing freedom to the others in 1799.

Our local churches even have separate booths or balconies, which, back in those times, kept the colliers apart from the rest of the congregation; and I still recall back in the days when I was a child, some locals—all be it just a few of the older ones—still regarded the collier as an underclass; almost like the untouchables in India … well, not quite.

At the top end of Mr Chalmers' allotment, which was about half an acre in size, is his pigeon loft, or doo'cote, built on top of a sizeable looking shed. Often, I would see him sitting on the veranda-type landing area, encouraging his flock by rattling a tin of corn or beans and calling out: 'Peas … peas … peas!' They would circle round and round in bunches of twenty or thirty, then gradually one after the other, land and disappear into the loft.

*Mr Chalmers in his allotment, at the end of Dukestreet…*

Across the street from Mr Chalmers' place is a property with a small orchard. I don't recall ever seeing the occupants of that particular place, but I did hear them once when I attempted to raid their apple trees. The roar from somewhere in the direction of their house sent shock waves down my whole spine. I don't even remember my exit from the place, it all happened so fast.

A short distance further up the street is Peter Hamilton's yard where he stables his horse, Prince. Peter Hamilton or *Pate*, as the locals called him, was one of the town characters. His business was delivering coal around town. He was a tough looking roundly built man with an enormous Victorian style handlebar moustache, and fancied himself as Mr Samson … without Delilah. He would be seen at the local gala days in the tug-o-war events, or lifting heavy things, and could drink any man under the table; so to speak. My Dad and he never got on. I found out much later that it had something to do with the abolition of the sub-contract system in the coalfields soon after the mines were nationalised.

Apparently, sub-contracting was a system where an individual takes out a contract with the coal company, he then employs several men to work under him. He draws all the wages from the company and pays each man his share. The men never knew what the contractor had earned, or the rates paid by the company. The system itself created deep resentment and suspicion as some of the contractors made huge sums of money at the expense of their fellow workers, and in some cases did very little work for it. Many contractors were actually detested more than some coal owners.

As a union delegate for the National Union of Mineworkers, my Dad played a part in the system's demise. He was an individual who campaigned vigorously against unfair practices in and around the work place; which of course created some degree of resentment among a few of the locals. I was never aware of this, I must say.

From my vantage point up at The Roundel, as I sat watching part of our town go about its daily business, I suddenly spotted a private car (a rare spectacle back in those days). I recognised it at once. It was old Dr Heatherton's. He appeared coming up the Look-A-Boot-Ye-Brae, and made straight towards his house at Wellmyre, near the corner of Port Street and Balfour Street … I wonder who he was visiting. Obviously someone down the Carse … another baby arriving on the scene, or a farmhand suffering some injury … perhaps a small child suffering one of the many common illnesses of that time … mumps … croup … polio.

I always got a bit apprehensive when my mother took me to see him at the Main Street surgery. Standing there in the room with all the instruments and the various shaped bowls full of bandages and cotton wool—and that odour of methylated spirits. Then there's the needle—*the hypodermic*! For an infant, that must be one of the most traumatic sights. Watching the doctor making all the preparations; seeing him hold the needle up and measuring the exact amount of fluid by pushing the plunger till a little squirts out from the point; rubbing the area of the skin with cotton wool soaked in methylated spirits—*horrible*!

Suddenly, the voices of John and Tommy making their way back shook me out of my daydreaming. They had loaded their hankies full of gooseberries giving us a few to try. They said that very shortly there would be quite a few more, and also heaps of brambles. They planned on returning in a week or so with larger bowls to carry them in. Andrew and I were instructed not to mention anything to anyone, it was to be a secret, and with that, we made our way back across the field and headed home.

My mother made short work of the rabbits. She skinned and gutted the lot ready for the pot. I don't know how she cooked them. I only know that they were very tasty. In a few weeks, John would bring home his harvest of Gooseberries, blackberries, and occasionally greengages picked from a special tree somewhere on the Kennet estate. He and his pal Tommy never divulged the location. All this produce was immediately turned into jam, and some was just simply eaten on the spot.

Some of the jam was used on tarts and after being baked in the oven, it gave the jam a slight toffee texture. I just couldn't get enough of my mother's baking. The tarts, fairy cakes, shortbread, and her dumplings; even the smell of the kitchen during the whole process was an additional little treat. Meanwhile, Dad's garden produced his favourite vegetables, mainly potatoes, cabbages and Brussels sprouts. However, there were on occasions little treats like strawberries, rhubarb and peas.

## Out For a Walk with Dad

Several weeks after the rabbit hunt, my Dad, for some reason, had a couple of days off work. After sitting in his armchair in the living room, studying the racing form in *The Noon Record*, he decided to pay a call on Mr Milligan the bookie. Mr Milligan's place was actually his own home along Alloa Road, just a short distance from The Square. At the same time, Dad used the opportunity to invite Andrew and me out for a walk.

As we headed off down past The Green towards The Square, we saw, just ahead of us, the familiar figure of Pete Hamilton sitting on his coal cart being pulled along by his old Clydesdale horse, Prince. He turned right onto the Alloa Road; apparently making his way towards the Brucefield Mine to pick up another consignment of coal.

*Pete Hamilton on his way to Brucefield Colliery…*

As far as I can recall, there was never any occasion when he made deliveries to our house. Our usual suppliers were Wullie and Jimmy McAinsh, two local entrepreneurial types with a finger in all sorts of projects around town, from pig farming to fruit and vegetable growing.

Our coal delivery was always 20 bags, or one ton to be exact. It seems that one of the advantages of working in the coal industry was the concession coal. With our abundant supply, a warm home during the winter months was something we just took for granted. Then of course, having a well-tended fireplace meant a plentiful supply of hot water.

After dad placed his betting slip with Mr Milligan, we headed off in the direction of Kennet village. As we walked along, we could hear strange noises coming from the field on our right. Large oak trees lining the edge of the field obscured some of the view. About halfway along, between the Square and the Blue House Lodge, we came to an open gate giving access to the field. The noise of tractor engines and the sound of busy people stirred our curiosity. We crossed the road to investigate.

As we walked through the open gate, we found a group of farm workers processing wheat sheaves in a very large timber wagon called a threshing machine. It was driven by means of a broad canvas belt, twisted like an elongated figure eight between a small drive wheel on the tractor, and a large wheel on the thresher.

*Dad, Andrew and I on a walk towards Kennet village…*

While Dad stood talking to one of the men, Andrew and I strolled about taking in the scene. There seemed to be quite a number of people of both sexes, all with their different chores; most likely itinerant workers, for I had never seen any of them about town.

A couple of men stood beside a shoot catching the grain in sacks. As soon as a sack was full, it was stitched up with string and loaded onto a cart. A long narrow table fitted with rollers protruded out the rear end of the machine. Every few minutes, a rectangular shaped bail of straw, tied together with wire, shot out through a curtain of canvas straps. They were then loaded onto another cart.

Meanwhile, round on the other side of the machine, a couple of workers with pitchforks tossed sheaves of wheat up onto the top, where another two or three stood catching them and tossed them into, I assume, the starting end of the whole process.

There seemed to be a lot of laughing and squealing from the female workers, especially the lass up on top of the machine. One of the male workers appeared to be trying to make her laugh by tickling her, and obviously succeeding. The whole atmosphere was alive with the noise of the tractor, the machine, and the occasional screams and laughter of workers. It was a scene I will never forget, and unknown to me at the time, would never see again.

This method of harvesting was fast becoming a thing of the past. As we progressed through the 1950's and 60's, technological changes were to alter forever a way of life. Some people say it was a hard life, and in many ways it was, especially in my Dad's line of work. However, looking back, I can't help feeling a sense of loss, and I'm sure most everyone looks back on their childhood days with a deep feeling of nostalgia. Today, that field edged with its dry stonewall and oak trees running along the perimeter is now a housing estate.

After a while, Dad called us over and we continued our walk along the road towards Kennet village, passing the peculiarly rotund shape of the Blue House Lodge. For a main road, the traffic was few and far between: a couple of pre-war model cars, the odd coal lorry, and the local busses. Traffic accidents were almost non-existent; apart from one very serious incident that happened around that time.

The location was the road junction at the end of Kennet village, near the Esso petrol station. Two cars had collided with each other killing all the occupants except for one: a baby. Local gossip had it that the mother in one of the cars anticipated the danger and threw her baby out the car window saving its life.

When I got to hear of the incident, I took a walk up to the spot to investigate. Several policemen were around the wreckage taking notes, and one was sweeping the debris from the roadside. It was a gruesome sight and one I shall never forget.

We eventually reached the edge of Kennet village. It was until recently divided into two parts: the first part was the row of middle class type semi-detached bungalows, and a little further on, just around the bend, are the single story terraced cottages built for the local miners.

A short distance passed the first few bungalows, we turned off and headed down a laneway. Dad mentioned that the house on the right was the home of Mr Bald, the mine manager (which was at one time the old Kennet schoolhouse). The house on the left belonged to Captain McCullough, the local army cadet leader, who I got to know later on when I eventually reached the joining age.

The lane descended towards the single-line railway track, and just over on the other side of the track are the clump of Scotch Fir trees that I observed from the hump back bridge at Pilmuir a year or so before. We then climbed over the timber stile at the end of the lane and walked along the track, negotiating our way across the railway sleepers.

Just ahead, we came to a fork in the line. The right branched off towards Kilbagie and Kincardine, and finally on to Dunfermline. The left led to a siding, servicing the Brucefield mine; my Dad's work place.

A hundred yards or so along the siding were some empty wagons waiting to be filled with coal, and just ahead on the left was the mine entrance. Small gauge rail tracks emerged from the mine opening and continued up the rise towards the sorting trays, and finally the hoppers.

As we stood at the entrance of the mine looking down into the dark opening, there suddenly appeared several hutches full of coal. They were like small bogies measuring approximately 4 feet by 3 feet, and around 2 feet in depth. They could in fact be described as miniature railway wagons. A thick steel cable ran the full length of the rise pulling them along. The cables themselves were simply placed on top of the loaded hutches.

I ventured a little closer, walking two or three paces in towards the dark passage. Dad kept hold of my hand. I didn't get far when suddenly a group of hutches emerged out of the darkness like a trail of evil grey monsters. Dad led me back towards the light.

We continued our walk towards the mine-head buildings passing several of my Dad's comrades. On the other side of the mine workings stood the small collection of offices. Dad told us to wait outside while he conducted some business inside.

As Andrew and I sat about waiting, we noticed that Pete Hamilton had already arrived and was in the process of loading the last bags of coal onto his cart. Parked beside him at the hopper was the lorry owned by Jimmy and Wullie McAinsh. They were already fully loaded and standing by while Wullie headed off to the office to complete the paperwork.

The *Cainshies* (as we called them) were, as I mentioned earlier, quite an enterprising family. Not only did they have a coal delivery business, they also had a couple of small fields around the district growing mainly potatoes, and occasionally things like broad beans. They also had a small two-acre farmyard at the top of Castle Street, just a few yards up from the corner of Main Street, with pigsties and a hencoop. I believe old Ja-Ja's place at the top of the Look-Aboot-Ye-Brae also belongs to the family (Chapelhill is described on the records of the 1940's as a market garden. Old man Ja-Ja's correct name was James M. McAinsh). As well as running his market garden, his usual job before he retired, was the district postman.

I can still remember how they never passed up an opportunity, especially when it came time to harvest their fields. They had a cunning scheme worked out when it came to hiring helpers for the potato picking. Perhaps it was a situation that started by chance; whatever it was, they made full use of it.

They would start their day with a few workers, and sometime during the day, some kids came on the scene and asked to join in *the fun*. The location of their fields may also have contributed to the situation. They were in and around town; in fact one of their fields was situated over the hedgerow at the bottom end of our Terrace, and ran the length of Geordie Gray's property. We just climbed through the hole in the hedge and we were there.

Now, at the end of the day, we would make our way up to the *head-office* at the top of Castle Street in order to collect our pay. The procedure was to form a queue. The official adult workers were first in line, followed by us: the youngsters. There were quite a few, ranging in age from five years to around ten. The rate of pay also depended on your age; for example, how young and simple you looked. I have no idea what adult workers were paid, but I know that our rate ranged from two or three pennies to as much as half-a-crown. On one particular occasion, I was handed three copper pennies. I remember to this day what happened immediately after.

As the potato harvest was around October, the late afternoon was already getting quite dark. I left the yard and headed back home. On the way, I thought of popping into Lizzie Gardner's tuckshop for some sweets; however, as I made my way down the long dark passageway towards the shop entrance, I found the place closed. As I turned, I met three or four other kids from the pay queue who had the same mission. They asked if Lizzie was open. I said no, so as we stood there in the dark passageway, one lad asked me how much I had made for the day's work. I opened my hand and showed him the three copper coins. Suddenly, one of the group brought his open hand up under mine, causing the coins to scatter. They all walked away laughing, thinking what a great joke.

Meanwhile, there I was on my hands and knees groping about trying to find the money in that dark passageway. I spent ages crawling up and down and never found a single coin.

Dad finally emerged from the colliery office along with Jimmy McAinsh. They were both talking about the new building construction underway just across from the offices. This was going to be the pit baths where miners could wash off all that coal dust at the end of their shift. It was like the beginning of a new era, the dawning of a new age. No longer would we see the parade of blackened faces strolling home at the end of a shift. This was to be a giant leap forward for civilisation … as we knew it.

On the way back towards home, Dad decided to take the short root down the railway track towards the hump-back bridge at Pilmuir. The fields on each side had their crops already well harvested, and some were already sprouting their winter crop of turnips, providing the cattle with a good supply of winter fodder, and for us, the material to make our Halloween lanterns.

I noticed some years later that certain people in other parts of the world made their Halloween lanterns out of pumpkins. We didn't have pumpkins. I had never heard of pumpkins until I saw the pantomime, *Cinderella*. Therefore, we used the next best thing: the turnip; actually, they were Swedish Turnips, or Swedes.

As we walked along the track, I looked onto a sight I would never grow tired of seeing: the Ochil Hills with their autumn colours, and soon they would have their peaks covered with the first winter snow.

We climbed up the steep footpath at the side of the bridge and stepped over the stile onto the road. As we made our way up towards the main road, we could hear the sound of the threshing machine still doing its work across the field, and way in the distance, just appearing out of Kennet village, was the familiar sight of Pete Hamilton's fully loaded cart. Also the McAinsh brothers' truck had arrived at the Square and turned, making its way up the brae and into Zetland Street. We arrived home just in time for tea.

# Chapter 6
# The Festive Season

Miss Duncan stood by her blackboard giving us the last lesson of the day. All the classroom lights were switched on due to the dark overcast clouds, and the unrelenting downpour, with occasional lightning flashes and rumbling thunder resembling a bombardment scene from a WWI war film. Some of the infants in the class were showing signs of concern; however, Miss Duncan gave her assurances that it was all perfectly normal, that we were no longer babies and had nothing to be afraid of. It was just one of the many wonders of nature; and anyway, we were all *safe and sound* sitting here in the classroom.

But, there was also something else contributing to the darkness, something just as natural, and something that happened on an annual basis. Since starting school, I was beginning to take more notice of time itself. Our day began at a certain time, and ended at a certain time, and things like the approaching darkness of winter got more noticeable.

With our grey Burberry type raincoats wrapped about us, we made our way home up the dimly lit vennels and down the streets, aided of course by the latest electric streetlights and other celestial aids (the few remaining gas streetlamps were gradually fading into history).

Shortly after sitting around listening to the *Children's Hour* session on the radio, an evening meal (or *tea,* as it was called back then) would be dished up for us around the kitchen table, it was usually egg and chips, or sausage and chips with HP sauce. If we felt a bit hungry later on, it was most likely a slice of bread and jam; or on special occasions, sizzling melted cheese on toast (main meals were around midday).

At the start of my school experience, my mother arranged to have my dinner at school—what a grim experience that was. After the school bell rang for the dinner break, we victims lined up outside the entrance to the dinner hall. An outside catering firm brought in the meals. Sometimes we would see the van arrive with the stainless steel containers, like insulated milk churns, or large flat steel pans with lids. There was of course no choice of menu, except that it did vary from day to day.

The week would start with a kind of stew, and the ever-present carrot floating in amongst it. Next day, there would be a rather grey looking mince, mashed potato with peas and carrots. Roast pork was my favourite, because a small serving of applesauce accompanied it. The fish, I just couldn't handle. I think it had something to do with the bones; also, back in those days, fish was way over cooked. Then for dessert: semolina with a dollop of jam, rice pudding with another dollop of jam, and of course, crusty apple pie with custard.

I suppose I should have been thankful for small mercies. Maybe my reaction was that of a spoilt child, or perhaps it may have had something to do with school regimentation. I just felt that I needed a break from the classroom environment. With a bit of complaining and moaning in my mother's ear, I was soon making the half-mile walk back home during the dinner-break.

Shortly after teatime, depending on the weather, we would make our way out into the Terrace to join our play pals. The early evening games generally started under the electric street lamp at the entrance to the Terrace. The other kids from The Green also chose that spot. Our favourite games were things like *Hide-and-Seek*, *Tag* or *Kick-the-Can*. Then of course, there were the more mischievous games like, *Chap-Door-Run* or *Ring-A-Bell-A-Bunkie*. The game started off with each of us in turn sneaking up to a neighbours front door, knocking on the door and retreating to the nearest bush or wall to watch the expression on their faces when they opened the door and found no one there … infantile when you come to think of it; but, that's what we were.

One cold late October evening while some of us stood around under the lamp, we saw someone walking up towards us carrying a large object the size of a football. A length of string was attached to it acting as a carry handle. We soon recognised the person carrying it. It was young Maizie Marshall from No. 7.

The object was her Halloween lantern made from one of the large cattle fodder turnips. Her granny (known to us as *Granny Marshall*, a tough hard working nuggety old lady) brought it home with her after she finished her last day at the potato picking. She helped Maizie gouge out the centre; the contents of course would not go to waste. Two eyes and a skilfully shaped mouth were carved out. The scalp was cut across to act as a lid and giving access to the centre where the small candle was placed. She was obviously very proud of it and we all studied it taking note of how it was done. The following weekend, we made our way down to the nearest field and had a go at making our own.

## Halloween Festivities

On Halloween day, some lucky kids were asked to parties where *ducking for apples* and *treacle scone games* were part of the entertainment. I had never attended anything like that; however, I did have an idea of what they were like from reading comics; especially *The Broons* and *Oor Wullie* in the Sunday Post.

The most popular activity during Halloween was guising. It involved dressing up in our mother's old cloths, plastering our faces with her lipstick, and putting on one of her old hats. The down side of that was shuffling our way along the streets in her old high-heeled shoes; it was just a wee bit exhausting.

The other little problem was knocking on the neighbour's doors in the hope of being invited in. If you were lucky enough, you then had to put on some kind of performance, like sing a song, or recite a verse. The reward was usually a penny, sometimes a little more, and occasionally an apple or a piece of toffee.

When the day finally arrived, we got together and organised ourselves into small groups. My group consisted of three lads: Stewart Hill from No. 1, Jackie Murphy from Balfour Street (Lochies Road), and Bert Sharp from The Green. They arrived at my place already dressed up in their costumes and looking quite a sight with their faces made up like weird demons from an unknown part of the universe.

We set off up Castle Street towards the Mercat Cross in Main Street. Word got around that that was the place to be because three public houses were situated around there: The County, The Royal Oak, and The Horse Shoe Bar; and it was general knowledge to some kids that a man with a couple of pints in him was apt to be a bit on the generous side.

However, the competition was tough. Some of the older lads seemed destined for the stage. No matter what I did, I just couldn't top the performances of Nortie Hogan, or the talented lads of the Barr and Airnes families.

It seemed the whole town was alive with other guisers wandering about in their get-up. Some of them, I thought, had quite a flair for the occasion. Their costumes were obviously worked on in advance: witches' hats, broom-sticks, and even paper masks. Some of them even had the turnip lanterns (I did attempt to make one, but it was a bit of a nuisance carrying it around—the candle kept falling over).

Now, when it came to knocking on doors, the whole mood changed. I was as nervous as hell. The door would open and our usual line was: *"Do you want any guisers, Misses?"* Quite often, the response was in the negative, which was a little disappointing. However, we'd eventually come across a willing victim who would ask us to come in: 'OK, lads! Let's see what you can do!'

We were ushered into the sitting room where we found the rest of the family gathered around the fireplace. Bert was the first, he sang a kind of nursery rhyme, Stewart followed with a song of sorts, but when it came to Jackie and me, we just stood there frozen to the spot. We just never really prepared ourselves for the moment.

Finally, Bert and Stewart were given a couple of pennies each, and Jackie and I were given a couple of toffees. I suppose you could say that that was my very first experience of stage fright.

## Bonfire Night

After the guising nights, it was time for the main event. The bonfire in the vacant paddock at the side of The Green was coming on. It was about ten feet high and rising. There were piles of dead wood from the woodland, and some old bits of flooring, and broken pieces of furniture. In the few days before the great event, Andrew and I made a wee hidey-hole in its centre. We pretended that this was Aladdin's secret cave, and that the magic lamp was hidden somewhere deep in the heart of it. When our parents got wind of it, it caused quite a bit of concern. They told us that a child from another district a year or so before played the same game. He or she had entered the bonfire hours earlier and had fallen asleep inside it. The horror that followed when they lit the fire, not knowing that a child was in the middle of it, must have been devastating. My mother went crazy when she heard.

A couple of weeks before the event, shops started stocking up on a variety of fireworks. All the lads loved the bangers and the rockets, while the lassies seemed to fancy the roman-candles, and cartwheels. The penny-banger, or the squib, was the more favoured because it added a bit of atmosphere to our war games. The rockets were also popular, but unfortunately they cost a bit more, ranging from three pence to sixpence, reducing our arsenal by quite a bit.

Getting the money from our parents to purchase them was always difficult. About sixpence was my limit, but sometimes Dad would help out with a little extra if we promised to do some tasks around the place.

*Bonfire night: down at the end of Castle Street…*

Some enterprising kids would think up all sorts of ways of making an extra penny or two. Carrying the bonfire Guy around the doors and asking: *"Penny for the Guy?"* was one of the favourites; and the guising itself could be quite a good little earner—with emphasis on the *little*. Another source of income popular with the kids was collecting empty lemonade bottles—if you were lucky enough to find any. They had a return value of three pence at the local shops. Also beer bottles: the Younger's screw-top variety had a similar value. However, some places seemed to begrudge infants returning beer bottles, especially the bartenders in pubs. They just didn't like young kids coming into the public bars.

November the 5th had arrived and I had managed to save some of my fireworks. Shortly after our evening tea, we made our way out into the dark early evening air and entered the vacant paddock. Some folks were already setting off their roman-candles and rockets. There was quite a lot of excitement with kids running back and forth letting off bangers and cracker-jacks, frightening the dogs and smaller kids.

The older people in charge of setting the fire alight appeared from The Green carrying what looked like a person in a very serious state, and in urgent need of medical attention. It was of course the Guy: a dummy stuffed with straw, an old pillowslip for its head, and a hat stuck on top. Some of the people were calling out: *'Here comes Tojo!'* Of course, I had no idea of the history of this particular event, or who this dummy was supposed to represent. I did hear my mother mention earlier the name, Guy Fox, the man who attempted to blow up the Houses of Parliament. But, some folks were calling this one, Tojo.

It was one of the older lads who enlightened me regarding the identity of this particular character. Tojo was the Japanese prime minister who was recently found guilty of war crimes, and subsequently executed several weeks later.

As soon as Tojo was placed on top of the pile, we began stuffing the bonfire with old newspapers. Then, someone called out: *'Everybody stand-back!'* After the final checks were made, we all set about lighting the paper. It didn't take long for the flames to build. Some parts were a bit slower to get started, but eventually all sections met up. The noise of hungry flames devouring the dry timber increased. I stood staring into the raging inferno, watching the frenzy of flames and sparks fly up into the dark starry November sky. The sensation of radiating heat on my face increased, forcing me to retreat further back to a more comfortable spot. The sight was awesome, and the excitement of everyone present added to this breath-taking moment.

Tojo was now well alight and as I stood looking up at the burning effigy, I paused, giving thought to what it must be like for someone to be burned alive like this. It looked a horrifically painful way to go.

The raging noise gradually died away just minutes after the fire reached its peak. Burning timbers started caving in and the once magnificently tall bonfire sagged into a heap of glowing embers. I couldn't help feeling a little disappointed. I would have liked the event to have lasted another half hour at least, instead, there we were, standing around this scene of gently flapping flames with maybe the occasional crackle of hot embers. A few of the spectators began drifting off home while others used the moment to cook up a batch of potatoes in the embers; a very popular activity around every bonfire or campfire in those days.

## A Visit to Our Local Kirk

School activities during the last few weeks before Christmas were taking on an air of pre-festive excitement, and one of the seasonal events included a visit to our local church. I particularly looked forward to it as it meant a break in the tedium of schoolwork. On the day, the whole school assembled out on the playground. Each class formed a line two a breast and then we all headed off through the playground gates, most of the infants holding each other by the hand.

We crossed over the main road and walked down towards the Pottery. We then turned left at the Masonic Hall on the corner of Kirk Wynd and proceeded up the steep winding road, passing Mr Mercer's property on the left and on towards The Merket Cross. We then made our way up High Street and filed in through the Kirk gate.

As we entered the Kirk, we were directed up a staircase to the pews on the balcony. From where I sat, I could see some of the local people sitting in their seats below us: old Granny Campbell from our Terrace and her daughter Mrs Small, and just to her right, old Mrs Dalrymple from Balfour Street; also sprinkled about the place were a few of the town dignitaries.

Everyone sat quietly along the pews, the only sound, apart from the sporadic coughing, was the organ playing softly in the corner. This was, for me, a rare occasion. I sat looking around at all the fixtures and fittings. The pulpit with a small staircase on each side, and an impressive looking canopy above it; and on the wall at each side of the pulpit, the various sized organ pipes.

After quite a few minutes of sitting about, the organ suddenly stopped playing and everyone rose to their feet. The Minister had entered through a small door on the left and climbed the steps to the pulpit. After the introductions and a short prayer, we began singing the first hymn. I didn't much care for all the singing of hymns and psalms but I did enjoy listening to the Rev Crouther Gordon's sermons. He definitely had the gift for spinning a good yarn. Of course, his stories were meant to teach us something, and in some cases they did leave a lasting impression; depending on one's views on life.

## Christmas Time

During the classroom art period in the days leading up to the Christmas break, the whole lesson concentrated on the making of decorations; generally coloured paper cut into links to form great long colourful chains, which eventually were pinned around the classroom walls. On the last day of school, we broke up an hour or two earlier. The decorations were taken down from the classroom and divided up among us.

The previous year, my mother attempted to decorate the living room as best she could. She somehow found a large branch from a pine tree and a suitable pot to put it in. It was placed in the corner near the fireplace. Over the next few days, she put her heart and soul into brightening the house up for the festive occasion with decorations around the walls, and she even purchased a colourful paper object that cleverly opened out to form the shape of a bell.

Then early one evening, Ma called us all into the living room and sat us around the tree (the branch). John was on my right, my mother on my left and young Andrew on her left. The pine tree branch stood in the pot in front of us. A few clumps of cotton wool and some pieces of tinsel paper were placed about it, also three of those round coloured balls … two were slightly damaged; probably happened during our move from the Lothians to our present home.

We sat there for a few moments looking at Ma's effort, and I felt an overwhelming feeling of melancholy. Young Andrew suddenly burst out in tears and said something like: 'Why can't we have a proper Christmas tree?'

His reaction took me completely by surprise. He was so young and yet he sensed the humbleness of the scene. As I couldn't even recall a Christmas before that one, how on earth did he know what one should look like? Anyway, from that moment on, my mother made sure she had enough funds to purchase a real tree and even some fairy lights.

Christmas Eve arrived and the atmosphere was electric. Ma and Dad said that Santa needed to know where in the room he should place each of our presents. Also, as he enters the room by way of climbing down the chimney, we should hang our socks on the mantelpiece so he can fill them with sweets and other goodies.

It was decided that all the main gifts be placed on the large square table in the middle of the living room. I jumped up and immediately chose the corner near the downstairs door so that as soon as I come down in the morning and open the door, there they would be. I got so impatient with the hours passing so slowly, I wanted to go to bed right there and then so I could wake up early enough to catch Santa.

We spent the remainder of the evening sitting around the radio listening to what the BBC had to offer. There were the usual carol singers, and a radio play like Dickens' *Christmas Carol*. Our supper was a cup of warm milk and maybe a small piece of toast. Soon the time came to head off to bed. I raced upstairs, leapt under the covers and tried forcing myself to sleep. Ma said she would stay up awhile to make sure the fire goes out. She didn't want Santa to burn his backside on the way down from the roof—I thought that made a lot of sense.

I lay in bed, my mind racing with anticipation. What else will Santa bring me apart from the particular toy I asked for? I began to feel a bit agitated and not in the least bit sleepy. I shut my eyes and tried to force myself to sleep. Moments later, I opened them and casually looked about the room. My attention gradually turned towards the window and I tried to imagine the scene of reindeers pulling Santa across the rooftops. Maybe, if I peep behind the curtain, I might be able to catch a glimpse.

I reached up and pulled the curtain back, but frost patterns were already forming on each pane of glass obscuring the view. My mind drifted back to that morning a year or so before when I got out of bed and saw Dad getting ready for work. How strange that morning was. Was that really in fact just a dream? Had I imagined that whole day? No … it was real … of course it was.…

I'm not quite sure what happened next, I was convinced I only had my eyes closed for about a minute or so, but when I opened them, something was different. Everything was quieter, and the light in the room had changed. The windowpanes were now thick with frost. Gradually, I became aware of the fact that I may have dropped off to sleep, but for how long? I crept out of bed and slowly made my way down stairs. The house was in complete darkness and not a sound anywhere.

I approached the living room door and gently opened it. I reached up for the light switch and turned it on. The scene that confronted me took me completely by surprise and left me standing with mouth wide open. The entire table was covered with boxes and parcels wrapped in bright colourful paper. My stocking on the mantelpiece was filled with fruit and sweeties of various colours. When I finally calmed down, I ran towards the bottom of the stairs and shouted at the top of my voice: 'Santa has been!'

My mother eventually joined us. The living room, by this time, was a scene of empty boxes and wrapping paper scattered everywhere. Our mouths were full of sweets and chocolate bars. It looked as if our parents cashed in on an entire year's supply of sweetie coupons from their ration book. There were Mars Bars, Cowan's chocolate-coated toffee bars, Boxes of Cadbury's Dairy Milk, packets of Liquorish Allsorts, Dolly-Mixtures and various other types of confectionary that were a gift from Grandma and Grandpa Stanton. Our Grandparents, being bakers, had made up a whole batch of sweets and cakes for all their grandchildren.

My present from Santa was a green scooter; in fact that year, all three of us were given scooters of varying sizes. There was also a small four-wheeled painted toy cart with colourful wooden cubes. They had large letters of the alphabet and small images of animals. There were games like *Hoopla, Snakes and Ladders*, boxes of marbles and decks of cards like, *Happy Families,* and of course, several children's books filled with stunningly coloured illustrations. We spent the whole morning playing with each other's gifts. Apparently, during all the excitement, Ma returned to bed to catch up on some sleep ... we never noticed. For me, I voted Christmas the happiest day of the entire year.

As soon as it was light enough, we stepped outside to join the other kids. There were a whole lot of cowboys running about the Terrace and girls with dolls and prams. Some kid's presents looked very elaborate while a few looked quite humble—especially the families with lots of bairns. One lad became the envy of the Terrace. Santa had brought him a pedal-car. It was green in colour with little headlamps and a small windshield. He sat in it and moved along working the pedals with his feet, the steering wheel completed the picture. It was a terrific looking toy, and I must admit, I was seething with jealousy. We all took turns pushing him around in it hoping he would offer us a turn driving it.

The young lad was Adam McNeill who lived on the corner opposite Mr and Mrs Mitchell's place. He was an only child, about the same age as myself and actually suffered quite an upset a year or so later. His mother was admitted to hospital. She died soon after.

Our Christmas dinner was held in the living room with a brightly decorated tablecloth especially fitting for the occasion, and for the first time, we had Christmas crackers. After pulling the crackers, we put on our paper hats. The main course was a small piece of roast beef with gravy, and roast potatoes with peas. The pudding was mother's own concoction covered with Bird's custard.

Although our family was not that interested in the royal family, we did catch bits and pieces of the King's Christmas message on the radio (I must say, I never noticed the problem regarding his stammer). Later in the day, we sat around the fire reading our brand new books. Some of the books had a little too many words in it for us to cope with, so quite often, mother would have us all seated around the fireside while she read to us.

Eventually, the perfect day ended. We still had quite a few days left of our winter holidays, and there was the approach of the New Year, which was for the older folks, the main event.

## The Relatives Call in For the New Year Celebrations

Several days later, while playing with my scooter at the corner of Castle Street and the Terrace, a group of people appeared from around the corner of auld Haerie Ferguson's place. I recognised them at once. They were our relatives from Prestonpans: Uncle Bobby, Aunty Annie and our cousins, Bert, Alex and Dan. They apparently came to see in the New Year with us.

I immediately ran back indoors to tell Ma and Dad. Moments later, the house suddenly seemed to fill with that distinctive East Lothian dialect. An hour or so later, more visitors arrived: Aunty Martha and Uncle Hughie with our other cousins, Margaret and young Catherine. There was barely enough room to manoeuvre in our small house.

A few minutes later, Dad and his brothers got themselves ready and headed off up through town to the Horse Shoe Bar, while Ma and our aunts put on the kettle for a nice pot of tea. Then I noticed that someone had brought a large rectangular tin container as a gift. There were no labels on it to suggest what it might be. Aunty Annie said that Uncle Bobby had acquired it through some pal of his. There seemed to be a short pause after that remark, and I couldn't help notice a slightly embarrassed smile on my mother's face. The tin obviously had something mysterious about it. It was the colour of green … army green. I for one was eager to know what it contained, but my mother insisted on saving it for later in the evening.

Meanwhile, the women settled themselves down in the living room with a plate of shortbread biscuits and a few slices of black bun cake—compliments from Grandma and Grandpa Stanton. We kids soon began to amuse ourselves with running about showing everyone our presents.

It became apparent that there was going to be a lively evening ahead. It was of course the last day of the year: Hogmanay. Ma, Aunty Annie, and Aunty Martha, were busy arranging the sleeping arrangements.

As far as I can recall, the front bedroom had a settee that opened out to a double bed, and I can remember that we had to position ourselves in such a way that some would lie with their heads at the top of the bed, while others had theirs at the bottom. As for the adults; that has always remained a mystery to me … where did they all sleep?

After some time, my Dad and his brothers got back from the pub carrying extra bottles of Younger's ale. He already had a box stored in the cupboard under the stairs; a little extra in case of emergencies. Aunty Martha and Annie had their own little concoctions.

In the course of the evening, I was wondering what happened to that mysterious green tin. Finally, my mother produced it and handed it to my Uncle Bobby. He placed it between his knees and with his pocketknife, prised it open. Inside were various assortments of American candy bars, packets of exotic looking nuts, biscuits, and things I had never seen before. I can only make a rough guess; those tins were intended for distribution to somewhere special—I never did discover the truth.

While the adults were all downstairs celebrating the last hours of the old year, we kids were upstairs having a ruckus time of pillow fights and scaring the living daylights out of each other with the usual ghost stories. Cousin Margaret had quite a talent in this particular field of entertainment. She would pick up a blanket, wrap it round her with just her eyes showing through, and making out she was some kind of zombie, or one of the walking dead. Now and then, the screams caused one of the adults to come up and investigate. I spent a great deal of time under the blankets.

Eventually, things gradually settled down, with just the occasional sounds of laughter from downstairs, and now and then, Uncle Bobby's gravel baritone voice singing verses from an old Al Jolson song. We soon drifted off to sleep.

Morning soon arrived. It was the first day of 1949 and of course, as usual, we kids were up and about before the adults. After much shaking of hands and wishing each other a *Happy New Year*, we made our way downstairs.

The remnants of the New Year celebrations were all too apparent. The table in the middle of the living room was covered with plates of leftover cakes and shortbread. Empty bottles of Younger's Ale lay about the room, and glasses still littered the sideboard and surrounding side tables. We helped ourselves to what was left of the cakes and shortbread biscuits.

Dan and Alec found a couple of beer bottles with some of the contents still in them. They poured some into a glass and began to impersonate our dads by acting drunk. I had a little taste, but wasn't much fussed with the flavour; however there was a particular concoction I took quite a fancy to. It was dark in colour and sweet to taste. Cousin Margaret told me that that was her mother's port wine, and that I shouldn't have too much, otherwise I would end up falling all over the place. Port wine … *El Dorado Port Wine.* I will never forget the effect after only two or three glasses.

Eventually, our mothers made their way down stairs and immediately chastised us for drinking the alcohol. Our fathers, it seems, were still feeling the worse for wear and didn't appear until much later. Gradually the cleaning up began and in no time we were all sitting in front of a warm fireside. Then suddenly, someone called out: 'Look! Look outside! It's snowing!' Sure enough, flakes of snow were gently falling. We kids immediately ran outside.

The flakes were quite small at first but gradually increased in size to almost an inch in diameter. We did have some snow earlier on, but it didn't last very long due to the wet ground; but today, the ground was dry and frosty, and within no time, a white coating lay all over the Terrace and on the tops of the lawns and hedges. We danced about in it feeling the soft gentle flakes on our faces. As soon as there was a sufficient amount on the ground, we began making snowballs.

The other kids in the Terrace soon joined us and the excitement increased. Snowballs began flying in all directions. Some of the neighbour's dogs joined in the fun, especially Tommy Flynn's dog Tito (apparently, it was named after the Yugoslavian President; so I was told). The whole Terrace was filled with the sounds of shouts, screams, and dogs barking.

Soon after, all the relatives got themselves ready for the journey back to the Pans. It was great fun seeing them all and I wished they could have stayed a lot longer. Dad walked down to the bus stop with them, while Ma stayed with us. We stood at the gate and waved them off, watching them making their way through the snow covered streets and disappearing around the corner and down towards the main Alloa Road.

Back inside the house, it all seemed very quiet. Ma immediately started tidying up. I sat down by the fire and thumbed through a couple of the Christmas books. The snow outside continued falling—not too heavy, just a steady pattern, almost perpendicular. If this keeps up, there will be sledging on the fifteen-acre brae over at Chapelhill, or up at the more adventurous slopes of the Tower Brae. I didn't own a sledge as yet, but John had one, had it specially made by Mr Drummond the joiner at the corner of the Cattle Market and North Street.

In the next few days, the holiday will be over, and it will be back to school. Soon, I will be moving on to Miss Pearson's class, and then to Miss Miller's the following year. When that eventuates, I will no longer be classified an infant. To mark the occasion, I will be moved into the *big boys* playground where some serious soccer is played, and even—for some—a bit of clandestine smoking behind the high playground wall next to the railway track.

# Part II

# Chapter 7
## Things Get a Bit Better

The tired and exhausted Labour Government of Clement Atlee, weighed down by the immense burden of war debts, finally lost the election of 1951, and Winston Churchill returned to *Number 10*. Dad was bitterly disappointed.

Another sad event happened closer to home, although for the people involved, it was a welcome situation. Families from The Green, were now re-housed in a new development down at The Pottery, which meant most of our playmates had moved over to the other side of town, leaving the gang numbers in a very sad state. The balance of power had suddenly shifted. The Zetland Street boys were now the dominant force in the area.

No doubt, for the families who lived in The Green, the chance of seeing the back end of those hovels couldn't have come soon enough.

Bit by bit, as the houses were vacated, we found ourselves with a new playing area. Some of the previous occupants had left the odd window unlocked and we lost no time in gaining access to the rooms, with some adventurous lads even managing to climb up through the ceiling trap door and into the attic.

For the first time, I realised just how small those cottages were, and the perplexing question remains with me to this day: how did some of those large families cope in such a small space?

Not long after, a few scavengers descended. The empty cottages were stripped of anything that might have been worth a few bob at the scrap merchants, or something useful like a few lengths of timber flooring, and maybe a couple of doors for the doo-cote, or bird aviary.

Between the scavengers and a lot of the local kids, the cottage interiors were reduced to rubble. The only thing left standing was the main support walls and the roof. I often wonder what it is that kids our age found pleasure in destruction—pulling things apart, smashing things to pieces. Of course, no one really cared what happened to the buildings, they were all earmarked for demolition anyway; but that behavioural pattern has often perplexed me. I suppose changing the trend from destruction to construction required a bit of education, a bit of effort in developing the brain.

While rummaging about through the area at the back of the Green, I happened to come across a popular sought after item; an old pram with its wheels still intact. It was almost hidden among the thick grass near the high perimeter hedge, the very thing I needed to make a start on my own trolley. All I had to do was remove the wheels and axles, and with all the scrap material lying about the place, there would be more than enough bits and pieces to make a start on the project.

Dismantling the wheel assembly was no problem. During the process, my brother Andrew turned up accompanied by a couple of our playmates: Stewart Hill from across the way at No. 1, and George McQueen. George was in Andrew's class at school. Up until recently, he lived in The Green. I got the impression he was very happy with his new home in Kersegreen Road. Actually, George seems to be, in some way, related to auld Haerie Ferguson, the old baker with the property opposite The Green. He even calls auld Haerie's housekeeper, Aunty Lille; although I'm not sure if they're related; it may just have been a bairn's thing.

Aunty Lille was a very friendly person, always offering a piece of cake and a cup of lemonade. I think the most striking thing about her was her healthy outdoor appearance and her very strong Highland accent—she was definitely not from around these parts. Both she and auld Haerie didn't seem to mind us kids playing about the yard, as long as we didn't frighten the animals; though mind you, auld Haerie's manner was still a bit gruff.

There was another man about the place, quite a young looking man, I'd say perhaps in his twenties, and again very amiable. His name was George, and I'm sure I heard young George refer to him as Uncle George. He would often give us some chores to do, like mix up a bit of pigs swill, or fill the pans with feed for the poultry. It was really quite good fun. Usually, it was just George, Andrew, Stewart and me. Most of the time we would run about the stables playing among the hay, or climbing over the large rafter beams and swinging off ropes.

On this occasion, George was visiting auld Haerie on an errand for his mother. He bumped into Andrew and Stewart as he was leaving the yard. They started getting involved with my project, and it was Stewart who came up with the solution for the front axle. I needed a nut and bolt for the front steering section; his Dad, being the proud owner of a motorbike and sidecar, and who is also a bit of an amateur mechanic, had a few spare parts lying about the place.

He raced across to his Dad's garage, which incidentally was in the process of being built with materials from The Green and other places. He came back with the very thing, including his Dad's hand drill for drilling the hole. All I now needed was the box. George suggested I try the sheds at the back of the Co-op in North Street, or just call into Joe Morrow's fruit and vegetable store at the top of the Cattle Market.

Actually, acquiring the box seemed to be no problem. With the Fyffe's banana box from Joe's place, I soon had my first trolley up and running.

My brother Andrew and I had hours of fun pulling it up the top of Castle Street in an attempt to see if we could reach the entrance to the Terrace. We didn't quite make it. The best we could do was the corner of Balfour Street, just opposite Dudley Hunter's general store.

After a while, some other lads from the neighbourhood joined in the excitement. They all wanted to try their skills at racing down the brae. There was Jackie (Plum) Murphy, Ronald Fyfe from Bruce Street, and John Patton who lived a couple of doors up from Jackie. He already had his own trolley, so we challenged him to a race. The whole event was quickly turning into a kind of racing carnival. The noise levels gradually increased and apparently got too much for the old lady living in the end cottage near the top of Castle Street. She came out and remonstrated with us quite vigorously. I thought she was going to hit some of us with her broom, so we eventually dispersed.

From that moment on, we unkindly gave her the name, *Granny Witchie*. This of course made her even more irascible. Her displeasure increased when the County Council decided to turn the small vacant plot beside her cottage at the corner of Izatt Terrace into a bairn's swing park. However, as it was basically a rock garden with a couple of swings, it never really appealed to us. We much preferred the park down the Cattle Market, or our most favourite playing areas: the Back Wood, the Kennet Estate, or up the Ladywood.

Over the next few weeks, we gradually added some modifications to the new toy. One day, while out playing in the vacant ground across our back garden fence, my brother John found another set of wheels from an old pram. They were lying in part of the ground set aside for the dumping of hard rubbish. Occasionally, some people threw out things like old armchairs or couches, and that would signal the possibility of hidden treasure in the form of coins lost down the deep crevices along the sides of the cushions. But, more often than not, the rubbish was generally garden refuse or things like old saucepans and articles too big for the *Bucket Rangers* to handle (Bucket Rangers was the name my mother gave the men who came around the streets emptying the dustbins).

Wheels were always useful and on this occasion, John came up with a bright idea. He used one plank of wood, attached the wheels to it, and used a single nail connecting it to the rear end of my trolley, turning it into a sort of trailer. This created a spot for another passenger.

A few days later, I came up with another idea. Lying on the rubbish tip, I saw an old sheet and toyed with the notion of using it to create a covered wagon, similar to the ones they have in cowboy movies. We used four pieces of timber at each corner of the box and draped the sheet over, tucking the ends down the sides. The trolley was now developing into quite a showpiece and we started parading it along the streets.

During one particular day, we headed off in the direction of the Look-Aboot-Ye-Brae. I sat at the front steering while my brother Andrew and his mate Ronny squeezed into the covered wagon bit, and Stewart sat behind on the trailer. Some lads also decided to accompany us on their bicycles.

We set off from the top of Ja-Ja's place at Chapelhill and trundled down the brae. I immediately got a bit concerned as we picked up speed, so I began calling out: 'Slow up! Slow up!' hoping that Stewart, sitting at the rear, would use his feet as brakes, but the trolley kept picking up speed. We had turned the first bend safely enough and were now at the steepest part of the brae. I took my feet off the front axle bar and scraped my boots along the road surface. By doing this, I was losing a bit of steering control, so I lifted my feet back on the front axle-bar. Looking ahead, I suddenly realised that if a car were to come around the next bend, there was going to be one hell-ova catastrophe.

Following just behind us were a few of our pals on their bicycles. They were yelling and laughing thinking it was all great fun. Meanwhile, the whole unit was going faster and faster. I managed manoeuvring around the second bend and shot passed the group of houses at the bottom. Then as I gradually pulled on the steering rope, it suddenly broke loose from the front axle-bar. All I could do was guide with my feet. Suddenly, we hit a small stone or a hole in the road. The trolley veered off to the left and struck the grass verge.

All I can recall moments after that was the sensation of tumbling through the air in all directions, sounds of screams and shouts of pain were heard. Then suddenly—thud … I found myself lying in a field and looking up at a blue sky. Andrew and Ronny apparently, shot straight through the sheet and landed close by. Stewart had leapt onto the grass verge just before the impact. The boys following us on their bikes thought the whole episode was very entertaining.

We checked each other out. There was not much blood, only a few bruises and scratches. I had sprained my ankle and grazed my hand. Apart from that, I was fine. We picked up the bits and pieces and started the painful walk back up the brae towards home. I spent the next few days in-doors with a badly bruised and swollen foot. The up side of the disaster was getting a few days off from school, which I took full advantage of by lying in bed until near mid-day.

## Local Entertainment

Around the end of the 1940's, some civic-minded people in town got together and organised a series of film shows up at the Town hall. It was to be run like a local cinema. My Dad took Andrew and me to see the first one. We waited in line inside the main hallway to purchase our tickets.

The film on that particular night was, *The Third Man*, starring Orson Wells. It was that famous Graham Green story about the black marketers in Vienna just after the war. I remember I was mildly interested, and strangely enough, the scene near the end where the character, *Harry Lime*, has his fingers poking through the manhole grate in an attempt to get out of the sewer, still remains in my memory.

There was another film I enjoyed very much called, *The Cat and Canary*; but the one that caused the most reaction was a Bud Abbott and Lou Costello film. Although it was classified a comedy, there was also the horror factor. Among the characters were *Frankenstein, Dracula*, and the *Werewolf.*

A bunch of us arrived early and managed to get seats near the front. Sitting beside me were John, Andrew, Stewart and Wullie Hill; and in the row in front of us, sat Charlie (Daz) Oliver from Balfour Street (Lochies Road), his younger brother Johnny, and a couple of others around our age group.

To say we were impressed by the shock element was putting it mildly. Each time Lou was in a situation where *Frankenstein* was about to grab hold of him from behind, a clamber of screams and shouts of: *'Look out! Behind you!'*

followed by us all diving for cover down behind the seat in front of us. Our mouths stayed wide open throughout the whole film. I think the Oliver brothers sitting in front of me actually saw more of the back hall than the screen in front of them. I could not remember a time ever before when I felt so scared. The utter relief we felt when the film finally ended. It was like having survived some horrific ordeal.

I was still in a state of shock as we made our way to the exit. On our walk home, some of us pretended to make light work of it, laughing and joking about how frightened some of us were. Of course, we all denied feeling in the least bit scared.

At home, I had a hot cup of cocoa and went to bed. The whole night was spent battling with ghouls and monsters. The nightmares were so vivid, I was sure the *Werewolf* was just outside my bedroom door, turning the handle in its attempt to get me. I woke up several times. My poor mother moved from my bed to Andrew's, gently shaking us out of it. Andrew, it seemed, had nightmares lasting over three nights. However, we eventually got over it and looked forward to the next picture.

Unfortunately, a month or so later, the town hall filming project was abandoned for some reason and we returned to bussing it into Alloa. Nevertheless, that was not the end of other ambitious community projects. There were the pantomimes: *Jack and the Bean Stalk, Aladdin, Cinderella,* and *The Magic Ruby.* This was my first experience seeing live theatre, albeit amateur.

The performers were mainly local people, and what great talent some of them had. The most memorable town characters were, Matt Hogan, a Brucefield coalminer, and Jimmy Pearson, a coal merchant from Bruce Street. Their comedy routines were a sheer delight. Usually, of course, they played the *Ugly Sisters*, or characters like the *Widow Twankie*, and ad-libbed with such natural skill, it made me wonder why they didn't try for a career on stage.

In early 1951, my brother John came home and announced that he would be performing in the town hall's next production, *The Magic Ruby.* He was picked to be one of the eleven soldiers in the chorus. The production would have over forty in the cast; many were kids from John's class at school: Wilma Small from the Terrace, and John's pals, Ross Kettles, Jack Adamson, Charlie Allan and many more.

The show would run three days, starting on the first Thursday in March and ending Saturday night. As far as I was concerned, I thought the show was a great success. John and his mates were all dressed up in their soldier's costumes with their wooden rifles on their shoulders, and singing songs while marching together in formation. It was all great fun. The band was Mr Milligan's Quartet and on the piano, Ian Rorrison, and a Miss Gibb. Two of the town's prominent citizens produced the show: Mr Masterton and Mr Duncan.

Most of the shows in the Town Hall were organised by Kirk activists; that is to say, community spirited people who came together through their association with the Kirk. Just a couple of years before, on July 1949, the Kirk put on a magnificent spectacle commemorating seven hundred years of the Kirk's establishment. A grand historical pageant held in a field in front of the manse. It was quite a major event with decorative ponies pulling small floats, and the main players dressed up in ancient robes.

It was through my Brother John's involvement in these activities that I was persuaded to take a more active part in the church activities. Sunday school was one suggestion.

However, the very mention of the word *school,* made me cringe just a bit. But, there were some interesting arguments in favour, and as a result, I decided to give it a try. So, one particular Sunday, my mother got me out of bed; although not exactly at the crack of dawn, a wee bit earlier than usual—that in itself was one of the downsides. Nevertheless, there was no turning back.

I put on my Sunday best, washed behind my ears, and strode off up Main Street towards the church hall. The church hall was a short distance up the High Street and down through a laneway on the right. As I approached the place, I saw a few of my pals, and a number of kids I never really associated with before standing outside the door. A woman turned up with a key and we all filed in.

Around the walls were various pictures of biblical scenes, and down the far end, a small stage. Eventually, we all settled ourselves down forming a semi-circle. The woman sat on a high chair in the middle and began to tell us about the baby Jesus. She went on at some length showing pictures from a book and got us to say our prayers … I couldn't wait to get out of there. The boredom was excruciating.

When I arrived home, my Ma asked me how I liked it. The twisted shape of my mouth, and the moan said it all. As soon as I changed into something more comfortable, I was off out. My mother didn't mind one way or the other. Religion was a subject that never cropped up in our house, although my Ma always said her prayers before she climbed into bed. I guess it was just the feeling of being in a classroom. Having to spend five precious days of the week in a school was more than enough. My weekends were precious. I had things to do.

Every now and then, I would feel like taking a day off from school—a shift off, as my Dad would say, or *plugging school* was another well-known term at that time. But, my mother was very strict when it came to taking days off school. I was reduced to putting on an act, pretending to be ill—a sore stomach, an aching head, or faking a cough. It very rarely worked. She would have none of it.

But sometimes, through a bit of clever acting, or it may have been that she just wasn't in the mood for arguing, I would have my day off; time at home to reflect and take stock, so to speak. Just sitting back and watching my mother go about her daily running of the house: making beds, beating the rugs and carpets, standing at the washtub scrubbing mountains of cloths on a scrubbing board, squeezing each item through a wringer and carting the whole lot off in a wicker basket to be hung on the line in the back garden.

Then every now and then, I would see her take a break from the daily chores and engage in a bit of gossip with the next-door neighbours. Generally, the meeting spot would be where our garden fence joined the back gardens of Mrs Mitchell and Mrs Reid. The sessions seemed to last for hours. Her other favourite break would be to sit herself down by the radio with a cup of tea and listen to her serials: *Mrs Dale's Diary,* or *The Archers*.

Occasionally, there were times when I would catch my Dad getting ready for the back-shift. This time he didn't have to wear his pit cloths to work. Several months ago, a brand new building was specially constructed at the Pit for bathing after work and each employee was allocated a locker with facilities for drying wet work-cloths. All he needed to do was arrive there and change into them.

This improvement in conditions came as good news to my mother. It meant that one of her worst chores had ended. No more washing heavily soiled work cloths, and no more would they take up space on the kitchen pulley. In fact, over the next few years, increasing improvements in the work place, and the growing affordability of household appliances would eventually herald the end of housework as a full time occupation.

# Dad's East European Odyssey

Dad's union activities seemed to increase year by year. He began by attending a number of conferences all over the countryside. One day he announced that he was chosen, along with half a dozen others, to join a delegation of Scottish coalminers on a visit to Czechoslovakia. Heading the trip would be the president of the Mine Workers Union, Abe Moffat.

This caused quite a bit of excitement in the house. The thought of my Dad heading off abroad—*abroad*! That was a travel experience reserved only for the well to do, and when I heard that they would be flying on an *aeroplane*! Well, the imagination just couldn't cope.

Now, as one of my activities at that time was collecting cigarette packets, I made him promise to bring back as many of the foreign variety as he could get his hands on. He said he would do his best.

The whole day before his departure got very hectic with choosing things to take on the trip. One item of clothing he had to hire: a Scottish kilt with the sporn. The tartan was Black Watch. Next day, we waved him off on the bus towards Edinburgh where he met up with the others at the NUM buildings in St Andrews Square. He would be away for two weeks.

At school, the teacher showed me on the wall map exactly where Czechoslovakia was. It certainly appeared quite a remote part of the world. I got the impression from our teacher, Miss Miller, that that part of the world was regarded with some derision.

Gradually, I got to know certain words like, communism, socialism, and a thing called *The Iron Curtain*. The area on the other side of this curtain was, apparently, enemy territory. When I asked my mother about this, she said I shouldn't go around mentioning things like communism to too many people, it'll just upset them … I was getting confused.

## The Shows Make Their Annual Visit

Two or three days later, the *showground* people paid us a visit. They parked their trucks, wagons, and caravans in the usual place: the vacant piece of ground across our back garden fence. Watching the first caravans arrive was always an interesting spectacle. They were all so brightly coloured, and similar in style to the gypsy caravans, only much bigger, and pulled along by a big truck carrying all their equipment.

*The shows across our back garden fence…*

Occasionally, we would potter about beside them hoping to be invited in to have a look around, but they never offered. Each day, a new attachment would be added. For instance, initially they would just have a set of steps leading up to the doorway, and a day or so later there would be something like a porch added on. They were the most interesting looking travelling homes I'd ever seen, not a bit like the holiday caravans at seaside resorts, and their doors were similar in style to stable doors. The bottom half could be kept closed and the top part left open to let in some air. Their community was so different from ours. After hearing stories about some people running away to join the circus, I began to toy with the idea myself.

It didn't take them long to get their stalls and roundabouts erected. In a day or so, all were up and running. The large generator wagons started up, and gradually hundreds of different coloured light bulbs and pipe-music filled the evening air. At first, I just walked about from stall to stall watching people roll pennies down small wooden shoots. Other stalls had one-arm-bandits, housie-housie, coconut stalls, and one with a row of clowns' heads that swung from side to side.

However, my favourite events were the dodgem-cars and the carousel with the variety of chariots and iconic shaped animals that bobbed up and down; but they were expensive, sixpence a go. With only two shillings in the pocket, tough decisions had to be made.

Some of the big boys often tried to snatch a free go by jumping on while the carousel was in motion, hanging on to the tubular barrier fixed to the edge. They were constantly being chased away, and there were the occasional accidents, some with bleeding noses as they slipped and fell down the steps.

Most of the time was spent just wandering about and enjoying the atmosphere, meeting other people, and playing with other kids running about the stalls. Two of my Dad's pals, Danny Young and Serge Aitkin approached me and asked after him. They wondered if we had received any news by way of a letter or postcard. To be honest, I couldn't remember if we had or not. One thing I did know, I missed him a lot.

The showground people stayed about a week, and soon the gradual dismantling of their stalls and roundabouts began. I always felt a bit sad looking at the vacant spots where only the night before there was such excitement; the sounds of squeals, laughter, and windpipe music still fresh in my mind. Eventually, the last truck, pulling its full trailer load, left the ground. I stood at our back garden fence and watched it head off. The whole area was now completely flattened. Well-trodden spots were clearly visible around the areas that housed the various stalls. The whole occasion certainly added a bit of colour and sparkle to our lives.

## Dad's Return

Ma said that Dad would be home by the end of the week. I couldn't wait to see what he had brought me, and what sort of exciting foreign cigarette packets there were.

At last, the day had arrived and as we got home from school, there he was, sitting in the living room with two of his pals, Danny Young and Mr Flynn from No. 8, and still in his travelling cloths.

Scattered across the living room table were all sorts of packages. His suitcase still lay on the floor and my mother was in the process of putting things away. I asked him if he remembered about the empty cigarette packets. I could tell by the look on his face that I was going to be disappointed. Then it was as if he remembered something. He pulled out one packet from his pocket, removed the two or three cigs that were still in it and handed it over. Sure enough, I had never come across this brand before, but the writing on the packet was in English, *Express 555*. I remember thinking that at least it was something. I discovered much later that that was one of the brands travellers purchased on the aeroplane … it was British. By that time, I had gone off collecting them.

Dad then said something like: 'Now, here's an interesting object.' He reached over and picked up a strange looking artefact. It was an elaborately carved bronze axe with a very long studded wooden shaft forming a point at the bottom. He said that it was a gift from the people of a place in the High Tetras, a mountainous region northeast of Czechoslovakia. He was told that it was a replica of a mountain climber's axe. To me, it looked like the sort of axe held by one of the guards standing outside the Sheriff of Nottingham's castle. It was a very impressive looking object and I wanted to run outside and show it to my pals, but Dad objected, saying it was not a toy. It was going to be displayed hanging on the living room wall.

The other object was a replica of a miner's Davy-Lamp with a presentation inscription on it. He immediately placed it on the sideboard. Initially it lit up by means of a small bulb and battery; but after playing with it for a week or so, the battery ran down. Replacing it was impossible as it was a special design and not available in this country.

There was yet another item, quite valuable. It was a presentation medal from the Czech coalminers. He reached into his case and produced a small black box. He pressed the tiny button on the side and opened it. There we saw a wafer thin twenty-four carat gold medallion with various designs of industrial tools and an inscription bearing his name in Czech: Willem Woodovitch. There was also a fine delicate chain with it. He was, I'm sure, very proud, and we were all very proud of him.

Within the next few weeks, there was yet another presentation. It arrived by special messenger. It was a large parcel full of photos of the whole tour and an impressive looking leather-bound photo album. Dad spent the next few days writing on the back of each photo a short description of the scenes. Shortly after, he glued each one onto the pages of the now family album. The notes on the back of those photos would not be seen again for another fifty years when I carefully dislodged them to be archived in digital form.

My Dad's involvement in the NUM brought him great respect amongst his peers, and as I mentioned earlier, it also created a number of enemies. However, his enemies were few, and of no real consequence. On many occasions, the house would be full of his colleagues and pals discussing union affairs, or just everyday working conditions. I would often hear terms like: *output tonnage, Check Weighman,* and *pit props.*

It was around this time I began taking an interest in politics, wholly influenced of course by my Dad. Socialism was the way to the future—according to Dad. It all sounded so simple. Wealth was to be distributed amongst everyone, not just the privileged few. I couldn't understand why some people couldn't see that; especially working people who didn't have much anyway. To a child's mind, it was perfectly obvious that some of us had very little, and were just getting by, while a few had more money than they actually needed. As I was to find out much later, things are never that simple.

# Chapter 8
# Crisis and Festivities: Sadness and Joy

One very cold morning around the beginning of February 1952, I was strolling with my usual enthusiastic pace through town towards school, when gradually I got the feeling that some sort of tragedy had occurred. I caught bits and pieces of conversation from other people in the streets. There were words like sadness, death, and snippets of things like: *"He wasn't that old, was he?"* I couldn't help wondering whom they were referring to, and as I approached the school, someone called out: *"Oh! Look! The flag's at half-mast!"* I looked up and saw the Union flag on the school building flying halfway down the pole … What did it all mean?

I entered the classroom and sat at my desk. Miss Hutchison stood beside the blackboard waiting patiently for us all to settle down. She was a stern faced woman with a demeanour that showed no tolerance for nonsense; however, on that particular morning she appeared calm.

She waited until the closing of desk lids and the clattering of chairs settled down, and then finally she said, 'Children …' There was a moment's hesitation, and then she continued, '… Children, I have some very sad news. Some of you may already have heard over the wireless that His Majesty the King passed away last night.' There was another moment's pause, and then she continued with, 'You may all have noticed that the flag over the school is flying at half-mast. This is a sign indicating the death of His Royal Majesty the King.' She also mentioned that as the King had no male heir, his oldest daughter, Elizabeth, would be next in line for the throne.

Some of the lassies in the class wanted to know if her husband, the Duke of Edinburgh, would now be called King. Miss Hutchison attempted to explain the protocol, which went way over my head.

But I did feel a sense of loss. Seeing the King on the newsreels at the pictures gave me the impression that he was a good-natured sort, there was something about him that reminded me of my own father.

There was a tune going about at the time and one of my classmates told me that it was dedicated to the King—it wasn't true of course, but it sounded appropriate. It was a tune played on trumpet by Eddy Calvert: *Oh! My Papa.*

The people in England appeared to be far more emotional about the news than most of us here in Scotland. My Ma and Dad didn't seem to give an opinion one way or the other; in fact, the only people who expressed any sadness were the so called upper class folks: the Minister of the Church, some of the teachers, and folks who lived in bungalows.

If there was any sadness amongst us kids, it soon vanished due to the government's announcement that sweetie rations were now at an end. Ma gave us sixpence each, and we went off to hit the shops. John was first out the door, and Andrew seemed to disappear without a trace. I headed straight up Castle Street towards Lizzy Gardner's shop.

When I asked for my favourite sweetie, she said, 'Sorry son, I'm all sold out of that variety.' I then made my way to Rorrison's shop down at the corner of Castle Street and the Cattle Market. The story was the same. It seemed most of the popular sweeties were all sold out.

The streets were full of kids, some holding large paper bags filled with all sorts of goodies. I called into Bell's the Newsagent, just a couple of doors up from the Town Hall. The only sweets left over were the sort I really didn't fancy, or they were the expensive sort. Finally, I called into the Co-op grocery store and stood there looking up at the branch manager. He just looked down at me and said with a smile on his face, 'Do you like Pan-Drops?' I wasn't really keen on Pan-Drops, however, as the situation appeared the same in most of the shops, I said, 'OK, I'll have a penny worth, thanks.'

I returned home and as I entered through the backdoor, my mother immediately asked me if I managed to get any sweeties. I showed her the small bag with the remaining Pan-Drops. She then said, 'At least, you managed to get some sweeties.'

John apparently didn't care for the ones on offer, so he bought himself a mouse-trap!

The following day I made sure I wasn't going to miss out. I made an early start. The supply man hadn't arrived at Lizzy's shop and I continued on up the

Street. At the corner of Main and Castle Street, I saw a van standing outside Bell's news agency. I ran up, stepped inside the shop and waited patiently while the deliveryman completed his paperwork. Finally, Mrs Bell asked me what I would like. I bought a Mar's Bar for four pence and a Penny Dainty.

From that moment on, the daily sweeties were our given right. The first stop on our way to school was the sweet shop, where, with our daily allowance, chose one of those, two of them, and a half dozen of the other.

The different types of confectionary seemed to increase as the months went on. There were—apart from the usual Dolly Mixtures—Jub-Jubs, Jelly Babies, and things like Lucky Tatties, Gob-Stoppers, and the Lucky Bags.

## Hospitalised

Maybe all this sudden change in the sweetie situation was the thing that contributed to my next experience. It happened one morning several weeks before my ninth birthday. I awoke with this awful nagging pain in my lower abdomen. I managed to gradually make my way downstairs, and as I sat beside the fireside holding my stomach, my mother appeared from the kitchen with some breakfast. She took one look at me and said with a suspicious tone in her voice, 'What's the matter with you?' As soon as I told her that I wasn't feeling too good, I could see at once the usual look of disbelief, and an expression on her face that said: "*Here we go again.*"

But the pain I was feeling added some strength to my argument; in other words, I was making more fuss than usual. Eventually, I was given the benefit of the doubt. I was then told to go back to bed.

During the day, the pain persisted and seemed to get worse. Late in the afternoon, my mother returned from her shopping up at the store. She then realised that this wasn't my normal playacting. Her expression of doubt had now changed to that of concern.

Later, when my Dad arrived home from work, both he and my mother decided it was time to fetch the doctor.

Dad immediately headed off towards the doctor's surgery in Main Street. When he returned, he said that Dr McTaggart (the new doctor taking over from old Dr Heatherton) would be down as soon as he has attended to his last patient.

Finally, the doctor arrived in his car. He was a youngish man of slim build. He sat himself down beside me and went through a brief examination, pressing my lower abdomen and so on. Suddenly, the mood changed from the calm doctor in control to a man with a mission. Even I sensed that the whole room now had a feeling of urgency. The doctor was issuing instructions to my Ma and Dad, then without further delay, he raced out the door and into his car.

My mother turned to me and said that I was going to spend the night in hospital, and that the doctor had gone to the public phone box at the top of Castle Street to call the ambulance. Ten or so minutes later, he was back and shortly after that, the ambulance arrived. We headed directly towards the Alloa General Hospital. My Dad sat beside me all the way.

The ambulance backed into the casualty entrance, its rear doors suddenly swung open and I was pulled out. A nurse and an orderly were already standing by with a trolley. They carefully lifted me onto it, and the nurse tucked me in. I remember quite clearly the colour and style of her uniform: dark inky blue with the starched white apron, and on her head a white frilly cap.

I was wheeled directly into the operating theatre. The place seemed full of busy people all dressed in long white gowns. The last thing I remember was the constant sound of clattering instruments in metal dishes, and a nurse trying to get me to pee into a bowl. A mask was then placed over my face, and within seconds, I was gone.…

It was dark. I was in a bed and the sound of a short cough from somewhere in the room stirred me. I opened my eyes a bit wider. A strange red glow shone from somewhere above. I turned my head slightly, and immediately, I felt a sharp pain on my right side. I reached down and touched something sticking out of my stomach. It was like a small piece of wire attached to my skin. I tried to pull it out but the pain was too much. I gave a short moan and heard someone in a bed next to me say: 'It's all right, son. I'm here.' It was my Dad.

The hospital ward we were in was quite large with rows of beds running down each side. The strange glow was a red coloured electric light bulb hanging from the ceiling. Then I saw a figure coming towards me with a small torch … It was a nurse. She asked me in a low voice if I wanted anything, and then she turned and said something to my Dad. The last thing I remember was the nurse adjusting my bed covers and shortly after, I drifted off back to sleep.…

There were voices … I could hear voices. My eyes opened on a scene so unusual. Nurses were talking and moving up and down the ward with things in their hands—trays, or pans, I think. I was in the same large room as last night. Daylight streamed in through the rows of big rectangular windows. There were people lying in beds. A nurse had noticed that I was now awake. She came over, said hello, and immediately began to take my temperature.

I looked across to where my Dad was and saw that the bed was now empty. I asked the nurse where he was. She said that he left early that morning. Eventually I asked why I was here. The nurse told me I was very lucky, and that they operated just in time … I had Acute Appendicitis.

The wire I had tried to remove from my stomach was actually one of the stitches across the surgical incision. There were two of them—thank God I wasn't successful in my attempt to pull them out.

I spent most of the day observing the various activities in the ward, and I noticed that I was the only youngster in the place. All the other patients were adults. Some of them sat up in bed with earphones on listening to the radio. I looked about but didn't see any at my bed. This was disappointing. I had never met anyone who owned a set of earphones before. I often saw soldiers in war films wearing earphones while communicating with HQ. This was exciting stuff, and I was dying to know what it was like wearing them. However, as a lad, I was painfully shy and didn't dare ask the nurse for a pair.

Sometime after the mid-day meal, I had visitors. My Ma came walking down the ward towards me with my brothers, Andrew and John. She had some brown paper bags filled with black grapes, and a few sweets. She also brought along some comics for me to read. They were a selection of American comics—I could tell by the cost in American cents printed on the front page; the figure followed by the cent sign, e.g., 6¢. Usually, they would be the Superman and Batman comics, and sometimes a few American war comics with images showing god awful looking North Koreans with thick-rimmed glasses and great buckteeth … those North Koreans looked an evil bunch.

I took the opportunity of asking Ma if she could get the nurse to give me a pair of earphones. She called one of them over and asked, but unfortunately, the connection by my bed was faulty, and as the ward was full, there was no chance. That was that.

The hours passed by so slowly and the comics were read repeatedly. Sometimes, I would just dose off until the visitors arrived, then one day I awoke to a number of colourful cards and gift-wrapped parcels. It was April the 1st, my birthday; I was nine years old.

The parcels contained a box of Dairy Milk chocolates, a selection of chocolate-coated caramels, and in one of the parcels, a big hardcover book: *The*

*Adventures of Rupert Bear*. All the images were in full colour and the stories were intensely engaging. The different characters that Rupert encountered were the small imp-like creatures he met in another world situated on the forest canopy, and his school friends: Bill Badger, Edward Trunk, and Algy Plug. I had hours of fun just lying there imagining myself accompanying him on his latest escapade.

There were certain nooks and crannies that I took mental notes of, and there was a particular boat or raft in one of the scenes that looked as if it could be put together with a little imagination. As soon as I get home, I'll set myself the task of building one. It all sounded so simple and straightforward, all I needed were the tools.

I was in hospital almost a week when a nurse came over and started dismantling a few things around me. She was going to move me to a different spot in the ward. Two nurses wheeled me all the way down the far end. It must have been the south end as it was much brighter due to the sun streaming through the window.

Then, suddenly, I discovered I now had a set of ear-phones beside me. The nurse set the whole thing up and from that moment on, I settled down to enjoying the BBC radio plays and music. I was thrilled to bits. There were serials like, *Lost In Space*, Brian Reece playing the bumbling policeman in *PC Forty-Nine*, Bebe Daniels and Ben Lyon, and of course all the latest songs with verses such as:

*She had dark and roving eyes and her hair hung down in ringlets.*
*She was a nice girl; a proper girl, but one of the roving kind.*

Or

*Sugar bush I love you so, ta-tara-ta-ta don't you let the fella's know, ta-tara-ta-ta ...*

After a couple of weeks lying in hospital, I was told it was time to get ready to go home. My stitches were removed several days before, and it was just a question of arranging transport back to Clackmannan. Fortunately, the ambulance took me back. The doctor stressed that I was not to be too active for at least the next couple of weeks.

I sat around the house for a while until I couldn't stand it any longer, so I set off out. My mother called and reminded me not to run about too much. I told her I wouldn't. The thought of that scar opening up with half my stomach landing on the road convinced me to heed her concerns.

I strolled down to my favourite play spots: the Curling Pond, and the woodland behind the wall where by now the height of the newly planted pine trees were almost as big as I was. I walked along the footpath towards the west driveway leading to the Big House.

Halfway along, I came across a large tree beside the field where several years before we hunted rabbits during harvest time. It was a cherry tree. Its branches sprouted out like spars on a mighty sailing ship. At that moment, I wanted to climb it just to see if I could reach the very top and pretend I was up there in the crow's-nest; but I hesitated, the doctor's last advice sounded serious. I would have to save that experience for a later day.

It was a strange feeling, wandering about when everyone else your own age was at school. I actually felt a bit lonely, and even a bit guilty. I didn't have to pretend I was sick to take days off school, I actually was sick … well not really sick as in not feeling well. It was an odd situation. All this free time and not able to do things … boring really.

After a few days, I rather wished I were back at school—in fact, after a week or so at home, I tried persuading my mother to let me go back. In the end, she gave in, but warned me not to play too many wild games in the playground.

After breakfast the following Monday, I got my school bag and made for the door. As I walked up the road towards school, I began wondering what sort of reception I would get from Miss Hutchison. Would she get on to me for being away so long? … I mean, I couldn't help it … I was forcibly taken away and put in a hospital … Maybe I could blame my mother for not letting me return to school sooner. Whatever the outcome, I was sure Miss Hutchison was not going to be happy.

The school gate was now in sight. Kids were running about the playground as usual. Some of my pals came over and asked me what it was like being in hospital. Some actually had their own stories. A few had their tonsils out, some had broken limbs, and others were taken away by a mysterious van that roamed the district picking up kids and carting them off to the fever hospital … what was all that about?

Soon, the school door opened, and the appointed staff member stood ringing the bell, summoning us all into our specified lines. I held back and joined our queue at the rear. Our classroom was the first room on the right and as I entered, Miss Hutchison was there standing by her desk. She looked across at me with a look of mild surprise and called out: 'William!' An uncharacteristic compassionate smile formed on her face. After a moment's pause she said, 'How are you William? Welcome back.' Then she began asking questions about my stay in hospital.

I felt a bit self-conscious by the whole ordeal. No matter where I looked, I was confronted with faces looking at me and smiling. This kind of attention left me with an embarrassingly awkward posture and I was relieved to finally reach my desk and sit down.

I don't know why I expected to be chastised for being away. I thought that a schoolteacher's main concern was generally about good behaviour and discipline. It seems life is full of little surprises.

## The Gala Day

As the weeks passed, things returned to normal. The special treatment I encountered on my return to school was now history and it was back to the boring routine of schoolwork.

During the month of May that year, there were two major events: the council elections, won by Geordie Gray (he won by six votes), and the other was the town's annual Gala Day.

The Gala created tremendous general excitement all round, especially for the local kids. Ma had just returned from the Co-op drapery with three pairs of brand new sandshoes (footwear for entering the sport events on the day). She placed them on sheets of newspaper and coated them with a substance called whitening. She then put them on the outside window ledge to dry.

A week or so before, the local pipe band had been busy practicing at their usual spot just outside Dudley Hunter's general store on the corner of Balfour and Castle Street. All the kids in the district couldn't wait for the big day. There were dozens of different events for all age groups, and even a chance of winning cash prizes. However, before all the sport events could take place, there was the crowning of the Gala Queen held up at the Town Cross.

A few days before, gangs of builders erected a great platform against one side of the Town Clock with large broad steps leading up to it. This would be the scene for the crowning ceremony. The girl taking on the 1952 role of the queen was Jean Campbell. I wasn't aware, at the time, just how she got herself picked for the honour. I suppose there was some kind of committee somewhere who made the selection, or some kind of election procedure.

*The crowning of the Gala Queen, held up at the town clock...*

Another small chore we had to go through before the event was the visit to Alec the barber up in Main Street. This, without a doubt, was a busy time for Alec. His small shop was full of customers; which left us with no other option than to call in periodically, just to check the length of the queue. Eventually, there was a spot on the long bench, and the waiting process involved a great deal of thumbing through the National Geographic magazines, and listening to the general comments regarding the up-coming event.

When the day arrived, Ma dressed us all in our best shirts and shorts. Our brand new dazzling white sandshoes added a special touch to the occasion. John, Andrew and I made our way out into the Terrace where we met up with all the others. We started walking up Castle Street in groups towards the assembly point down at the public school. Our parents, making their own way, weren't far behind.

Down at the public school, we were ushered into position for the march towards the Town Clock. The Clackmannan pipe band struck up the first tune and moved off, leading the parade along Alloa Road.

Following directly behind the band were two horse drawn coaches: the first carried the Queen and Master of Ceremonies, the second, the Ladies in Waiting, and parading directly behind them were all the youngsters of the town.

A short distance along, after passing Harrower's tuck-shop at the intersection where the road leads down to the mill, we turned right and headed up the steep Cattle Market and on towards The Cross.

As we walked up Main Street, I could see that quite a crowd had gathered. There were people from the outlying farms and villages, and I even noticed one or two of our schoolteachers. When the band arrived at the town clock, they peeled off, allowing the coaches access to the drop off point where the royal entourage disembarked.

We began running about the crowd with great excitement, bumping into kids I barely recognised due to their slicked-back Brylcreemed short hair, and dressed in cloths that actually outdid their Sunday best. Everyone began jostling about in an attempt to get a good viewing spot.

Up on the platform, the speeches came thick and fast. Miss McCowan, one of the teachers from our school, stepped forth, dressed in a dark blue outfit with hat to match and uttered her prepared formal address. This was followed by other little speeches from the young man who acted as the Master of Ceremonies. Then shortly after that, the actual crowning ceremony.

Minutes later, the Master of Ceremonies gave permission for certain persons to make their approach and pay homage. They included young representatives from the WRENS, WRAC's, and a few other junior organisations. The whole event was concluded by a troop of eight young lassies dressed in kilts doing highland formation dancing. After that, it was all systems go for the games down at the public swing park at the bottom of the Cattle Market.

After yet another round of short speeches from the purpose built timber platform erected down at the park, the games began. There were Highland Dancing competitions, and bagpipe competitions, and finally the events we were all waiting for—the track events, each categorised by age group.

First prize was something like a half-crown, second was one shilling and sixpence, and the third was sixpence or nine pence.

*After the crowning event, it was all systems go the swing park...*

I must say, I can't ever remember winning a first prize. I was never much of an athlete, but I did on rare occasions get a second; generally, it was third prize (perhaps, that year I wasn't quite fit enough, due to the hospital experience).

The various events were, the three-legged race, egg and spoon, wheelbarrow, and on to the older kids full track circuit. There was of course the greasy-pole, or climbing the rope, and for the adults, the *tug-o-war*.

Whatever the outcome, the Gala organisers made sure that no child went away empty handed. About halfway through the day, an announcement was made that the time had come for the distribution of *The Lucky Bags*. All the youngsters were to line up and receive a small paper bag (usually filled with something like fruit, sweets and chocolates, also a small bottle of lemonade). At the end, of what was for me, a fantastic occasion, the grounds gradually emptied and soon we all headed back home—except for the event winners who headed straight for the sweetie shops.

# Chapter 9
# Battlements, Bombs and Bullets: Our Theatre of Action

The summer break had arrived and spirits were high. Our usual games had evolved from cowboys and Indians to commandos. Our imaginary firearms progressed from six-shooters to Sten guns and Tommy guns, fashioned out of branches from small dead trees, or old pieces of timber.

The enormous number of young fir trees planted only a few years before down at the Plantation had grown just over our heads, giving us enough cover to take our enemy by surprise, and them us. Adding to all that, the sound effects of rapid machinegun fire created by yelling: *"Eh, eh, eh, eh, eh ..."* gave the atmosphere that extra touch of drama. Some of the death scenes were worthy of an Academy Award.

The Plantation—our theatre of action—is a U-shaped stretch of ground. The inner part skirts the edge of the field where, during harvest time, there is the opportunity to catch a rabbit or two. It curves past Ja-Ja's place at Chapelhill and continues running along the edge of the south field behind The Roundel, (the circular enclosure full of bramble bushes and gooseberries, situated on the rise) and ending near Kennet House. The outer part runs from about the Blue House Lodge (gatehouse to the estate) along passed the curling ponds, and down the Look-Aboot-Ye-Brae at Chapelhill. It then turns east along a narrow farm road and joins the other half, near Kennet House.

For me, the most intriguing part of the Plantation lies at the bottom of the Look-Aboot-Ye-Brae, just before the perimeter wall turns along the narrow farm road. A small doorway with a Romanesque style arch lintel opens directly into the plantation. Three or four stone steps lead up from the roadside.

The door—in those days—was made of heavy oak-timber, and covered with black cast iron studs. A large ring shaped door handle gave it that old medieval look. To my young mind, the whole atmosphere of the place filled me with a sense of foreboding, as if it were saying: *"Enter here at your own pearl!"*

*A small doorway opens directly into the plantation…*

Most of the time the door remained locked, however, some older lads managed to pick the lock—which I discovered later, wasn't that hard to do. The keyhole was enormous, and the key itself must have been the type as seen around the belt of a medieval gaoler; consequently, fiddling with a piece of strong wire through the hole and sliding the locking lever across needed no great knowledge in burglary skills.

Once opening the door and passing through to the other side, you find yourself standing before a pathway wide enough for a horse and carriage. The pathway winds its way up a gradual incline through the trees, and ends up at an old iron gate leading to the estate's west drive. The main entrance to Kennet House was just a short distance further on.

Another gateway on the south edge of the plantation gives access to a fair sized field edged with trees, and in the centre of this field are a small circular group of trees. According to some locals, that spot was used as a sort of retreat for the gentry of the estate. Apparently, the tiny circular woodland oasis had an attractive summerhouse in its midst. I must say, I saw no sign or remains of any when I wandered about the place; though it wouldn't be hard to imagine it. It was a peaceful little spot. In fact, the whole area was full of enchanting little peculiarities that stirred the imagination.

One day, while on one of my many solitary wanderings, heading aimlessly off down the Look-Aboot-Ye-Brae, I happened to notice that the old timber door in the wall was slightly ajar. I climbed the stone steps and cautiously pushed it open. The loud creaking sound from the hinges created an atmosphere similar to a scene from an old Dracula film. After a moment or so, I edged my way through and found myself standing before the familiar sight of young fir trees … what an anti-climax. I expected a much more interesting scene.

As I stood just inside the doorway looking up the wide track leading through the young trees, I suddenly remembered one of my earlier visits to this spot. It was a few years ago while out walking with my Dad. The trees were much taller then and of a far more interesting variety, their enormous roots spread out like muscular tentacles, and their branches were thick with leaves of all shapes and sizes. Shortly after that, the lumberjacks arrived in the district and began cutting them all down.

It seemed, even to my infant mind, that we had lost something; the ambience of a large enchanted forest. People from the town were always taking their Sunday walks through it, and the sounds of voices and laughter filtering through the trees, gave the whole scene an atmosphere of mystery, like the sounds of ghosts from the distant past.

After the lumberjacks completed their assignment, there was nothing but devastation. It took several months for the workmen to clear the area and make ready for the new trees. Although the Forestry Commission planted two species of trees, I could only recognise one lot: fir trees, or pines—anyway, they looked like Christmas trees.

## Charlie, The Lumberjack's Son

Thinking of the lumberjacks back then reminded me of a sad story involving a young lad that joined our class at school. One morning, our teacher introduced him to us; he was to be our new classmate. His name was Charles Reek, the son of a lumberjack. I would see him arrive each day looking just a little bit under the weather. His face had a pale sickly look about it, and he was always using his hankie. Over the next few weeks, the class gave him the nickname: *Seekie*

*Reekie.* We thought it quite amusing, and I must admit, I did laugh at this boy's poor condition.

However, it soon became apparent that Charlie was certainly not a well young lad. The amount of days he had off school were way above the average. Then one day as I made my way across the playground and out through the large wrought iron gates, I noticed him sitting on the perimeter wall. He said hello to me, and before long, we began chatting about things in general. I asked him what it was like being the son of a travelling lumberjack, and where about was his caravan. I said something like: 'It must be quite exciting living in a big caravan, and able to travel from place to place.'

We moved off together along the main Alloa Road. It wasn't my usual way home, but I thought … well, it's only a little out of my way. We passed the Railway Station at the bottom of Izatt Terrace and soon ended up at the intersection near the Square. I was just about to head up the brae towards home when suddenly he said, 'Would you like to come home with me and see where I live?' Reluctantly I agreed.

We walked slowly along the way towards Kennet village. At the end of the last row of houses, and just past the Esso garage at the fork in the road, we crossed over and headed in the direction of the Kilbagie Paper Mill. A short distance along the road on the right, we entered an area through a large timber gate where several caravans were parked. They were the same type of timber caravans that the gypsies have, only not so colourful, a sort of battleship grey. A small sawmill with a couple of rough timber sheds were situated close by.

Charlie approached his caravan and he called out to his mother inside. She soon appeared at the stable type doorway. There was a bit of an atmosphere and I sensed I was not welcome inside. Charlie turned to me and said, 'I'll see you tomorrow.' I watched him ascend the steps at the rear of the caravan and disappear inside.

Next day at school, he didn't show up. The whole week had passed and still there was no sign of him. Then one morning the teacher announced that she had some sad news. Charles Reek had died the day before.

## The Berry Pickers

I sat on the dry stonewall at the north edge of the south plantation, accompanied by the rest of the combatants, now fully recovered from the mayhem and slaughter. The conversations started taking on a more peaceful aspect, like: what our mothers had planned for our tea, or who was the latest neighbour to have a television set, and where was our next theatre of action going to be.

It was during this pause that we heard the sound of a tractor coming from somewhere in the direction of the Big House. At first, we couldn't see it, and then suddenly there it was, emerging from behind a large rhododendron bush, and pulling a trailer full of people. Sitting at the wheel of the small Davie-Brown was the unmistakable figure of Joe the Gerry, his cloth cap cocked to the side of his head.

One of our lads pointed out that they must be the workers knocking off from the berry picking down at the estate's gardens. They were mainly women and a few youngsters, all clad in their farm working attire: strong boots, trousers, or dungarees (most likely their husbands cast-offs) and of course the ubiquitous head scarf.

Every large estate in the British Isles had its own garden, providing various delicacies for the gentry's table, and the Bruce estate was no exception. After the Bruce family vacated the estate—about seven years after the 6th Lord Balfour of Burleigh died in 1921—the house and the grounds were rented out. The present lease holders were now the Alloa Co-operative Society; they took over the place in 1946.

The produce from the estate was now part of the Co-op assets. The gardens produced crops of mainly raspberries, gooseberries and blackcurrants; and during the summer-break, there were opportunities for some young kids to make a little extra pocket money. Some were even lucky enough to work on the local farms where the enormous sums of three or four shillings a day could be earned.

The berry picking was always the easiest work to find, especially for us youngsters; however, the rewards were certainly not the best for the time spent. Filling the small bucket with the berries depended on how quick you worked. I always found the whole process very tedious. Some of the adult workers appeared to fill their containers in no time at all. And Joe the Gerry, I noticed, had the knack of filling his bucket in record time. I was lucky if I earned three pence or four pence an hour.

Still, half-a-crown or so a day could buy quite a lot of chocolates and toffees. At the end of the day, if you hadn't already got bored with the whole thing and shot off home, a farm tractor and trailer would be available to cart you all home.

As I sat watching the people on the cart disappear down the brae towards the Gatehouse Lodge, and on towards town, we began making the homeward trek across the fields. Some of us talked of spending the next few days swimming up the Dead-Man's-Hole or Linn Mill. However, as it happened, word got around that someone had made a big rope-swing up near the tower. At the earliest opportunity, we headed off through town and on towards the old tower at the top of King's Seat Hill.

## Adventures in the Tower

The view of the surrounding district from the top of King's Seat Hill is a sight I will never grow tired of. To the north, the Ochil Hills stretch all the way from Stirling to beyond Dollar; and to the south, the spectacular sight of the great winding River Forth as it meanders passed Kennetpans, and on under the Kincardine Bridge towards the North Sea.

The tower, during the early 1950's, was in a bit of a sad state. A few years before, part of the east side collapsed due to mining subsidence. A tall cyclone fence was hastily erected to prevent the curious from sustaining a serious injury.

On the west side of the tower, and running along the south ridge of the adjoining field, are several tall trees. It is here that a few of the older lads managed to climb one of the trees, tying a thick rope around one of the branches to make a swing. When we arrived at the spot, there were already a crowd of kids standing around waiting their turn to have a go on it. A large knot at the end of the rope gave enough support for sitting.

After a while, I picked up a bit of courage and jumped on. The thrill of being propelled up into the air was an exhilarating experience; like swinging through the jungle in an old Tarzan movie. Then the realisation that the tree, situated on the ridge of a very steep slope, made the height from the ground at the swings farthest point seem terrifyingly high. Some of us remarked that if the rope were to work its way loose from the branch, there would be hell to pay. Some even speculated where you might actually end up … in the courtyard of Craigrie Farm, five hundred yards down at the bottom of the brae?

*Rope swinging up on the Tower braes…*

Finally, a few of us had had enough and we began heading back towards town. As we approached the tower, we happened to spot two or three lads moving about inside it. We moved closer to investigate. Then, one of them appeared at the first floor window. We called out to him and asked how he managed to get through the wire fence. He immediately pointed to a spot where you could crawl under it.

We were soon inside the perimeter fence and the excitement of being able to explore this ancient edifice thrilled me to bits. We tried opening the small door at the west wall, but it was firmly locked. The lad in the tower then pointed to an open window beside the door, but it was a bit difficult to reach. However, some of us remembered the technique the older lads used to scale the Rev Dr Gordon's garden wall during that disastrous raid on his pear tree several years back, so we gave it a try. I stood with my back to the wall and clasped my hands together while the rest climbed up onto the window ledge. They then hauled me up.

We found ourselves in a small room with an open doorway leading to a wide staircase that descended to the ground level. A spacious flagstone hallway ran from what was the front entrance (at the time completely destroyed by the subsidence and held up in places with steel scaffolding) straight through to the small door on the West side.

Open doorways in the hallway lead off to the left and right. The small room to the left, if entering the tower from the front entrance, was dark and full of rubble. We were told later by one of the local lads that this room once had access to a secret tunnel leading all the way to the Alloa tower, and that a mysterious incident took place:

Years ago—so the story goes—the tunnel was infested with hordes of avaricious rats, and access to the adjoining tower at Alloa became too hazardous. The local pest exterminators tried everything without success. Finally, a stranger approached dressed in full kilt and carrying a set of bagpipes. He proposed to enter the tunnel playing the pipes all the way along its length—it was thought the sound would set the terrified rats fleeing in their droves straight out the other end.

On the appointed day, crowds of people gathered. Some took up positions around the exit at the Alloa end, standing behind barriers for fear of being overrun by the panic stricken rats. The piper stood by the entrance at the Clackmannan tower, blew into his pipe and began playing. As he set off, the crowd let out a cheer.

Not long after, the sound of the pipe gradually faded into the depths of the tunnel. The hours past and still there was no sign of the rats emerging from the other side … not even the piper himself. Some said that they could still hear the faint sound of bagpipes coming from somewhere inside the tunnel; but others said it was only the wind.

A call went out for volunteers to enter the tunnel in search of the poor unfortunate sole, but volunteers appeared to be in short supply. The months and the years passed, and still not one person would dare enter the tunnel. The mystery of what actually occurred on that particular day soon evolved into a local legend.…

When I first heard the story, I shuddered each time I passed that opening to the small room. However, I was only a kid, and during my childhood days, there were many such fantastic stories circulating around the sitting room firesides.

The other room to the right was large and not quite as dark. The only source of light came trickling through a long narrow window on the east side. We all assumed that this must have been the dungeon where prisoners would be chained up around the walls and suffering all sorts of uncomfortable experiences … or maybe it was just the storeroom.

A small opening at the northwest corner gave access to a tight spiral staircase allowing just enough room for two people to squeeze past each other. We cautiously moved up the well-worn stone steps, holding onto the centre shaft. Small narrow slit windows lit our way until we reached the first landing that opened up into a large room. A fair sized window looked out over the town. The view was very interesting showing quite clearly the church and the clock tower down at the cross—we couldn't wait to reach the top ramparts, so we continued on up the spiral staircase.

The second landing led into, what was perhaps, the Great Hall. It was similar in size to the one below, except that the ceiling was much higher—this was because the upper floor was missing. The large cavities that once housed the thick timber bearers supporting the upper floor were clearly visible halfway up the wall, also the rafter beams above that were also visible. And perched along some of the supporting timbers were a number of pigeons.

We also noticed that this upper missing room had an intriguing observation gallery with three small windows facing north. We did our best to reach it but without success. Later, we would use a long plank of timber with footholds nailed into it. The view from that small gallery of the surrounding district and the Ochil Hills beyond was well worth the effort.

Continuing up the stairwell and passing the precarious opening to the room without its timber floor, we eventually ended up on the small west battlement. This sudden exposure to the exterior was scary. I stood by the doorway looking out onto the River Forth and over towards Stirling further upstream.

*On the top ramparts looking out…*

Although the day was relatively calm, the wind from this elevation pulled and tugged, causing me some concern. I stood frozen by the doorway in a sort of semi panic, holding onto anything and everything. The west battlement was not the actual top of the tower. The top battlement is just ahead, round to the left through a small doorway, and up another short flight of stairs.

In front of me, the base along the battlements sloped quite steeply; channels fell into large openings along the parapets allowing rain to run off. Through these gaps, I could see the ground directly below. I was gripped with fear. Some of the older lads made their move and ascended the small stairway to the top. They looked down from the top parapet encouraging us to follow.

One by one, we moved slowly across towards the small doorway. One of our lads decided to get down on all fours and crawl across. I followed his example. Soon we had reached the door and climbed the short ascent to the top.

After a minute or so, I gradually calmed down and took in the scene. It was indeed a spectacular sight. Almost the whole extent of the River Forth could be viewed all the way from Stirling, passing Kincardine, Grangemouth and Bo'ness. Standing on the south battlement and looking to the east, we could see the Kirk and town centre, but as soon as I saw the loose stonework hanging over the gapping precipice, and ready to collapse at any tick of the clock, I gingerly made my way back to a more secure spot.

The occasional visits to the tower over the next few years became more carefree, although I was still very apprehensive about climbing to the top battlements. Looking back on it, not one of us young rascals realised the incredible risks we took. If part of the east side had collapsed due to mining subsidence only a few years before, the thought of another collapse—looking at it from an adult's perspective—was just too horrible to contemplate.

## Panic Stations at the Seaside

At a particular time of year, there were the frequent trips to the seaside, organised by groups of people from local clubs and pubs. The destinations were usually some beach resort like, Ayr, Largs or Portobello. The accessories would include bucket and spade, swimming costume, and a towel. As for the adults, they were not that fussed. The women would bring along their knitting and suitable footwear for walking on the sand; and for the men, a hankie big enough to cover their bald patches, or they just made do with their cloth caps, and perhaps a little refreshment for the journey.

When arriving at the chosen location, I couldn't wait to hit the beach; but, the first item on the day's outing included a meal at the local tearooms. Sitting around restaurant tables waiting to be served was, for me, a very dull experience. Eventually, the first course would arrive: soup, then the main course, fish or steak pie. I actually quite enjoyed the steak pie, and of course loved the ice cream and trifle.

Then after that, it was all systems go for the seaside. We quickly changed into our swim gear and ran wildly about the water's edge. Some of the adults found themselves deckchairs and sat about chatting. The men would eventually retire to the nearest pub as soon as they felt that a reasonable time was spent with the family.

It was on one of these excursions—due to one of my many I adventures—that I caused a bit of excitement that might have ended in tragedy. The occasion was a trip to the Angus coastal town of Carnoustie, about ten miles east of Dundee. The patrons of the Horse Shoe Bar (my dad's favourite pub) organised the whole occasion.

The day was perfect with hardly a cloud in the sky. After spending some time on the beach, I got to the stage where I had enough of the paddling, and the attempts at sand castle building. I joined the adults and sat on a towel next to my mother. It wasn't long before I started getting a bit bored and decided to go for a stroll along the beach on my own.

I meandered along the sand doing a bit of *Beach-combing*. There were shells of all shapes and sizes scattered about, each with interesting colours and patterns. Bits of driftwood smoothed off by the constant pushing and pulling of the tide. Then quite some distance along the shore, I came across a fenced-off area. The fence ran in a straight line down towards the shoreline. Its condition was in a very poor state and gaps were present in various parts of it.

My curiosity got the better of me. I thought the area mustn't be that restrictive with so many gaping holes up and down its length, so I made my way through one of the gaps and continued along the beach. A short distance in, I saw some curious objects lying scattered about the sand. They looked like oversized dart feathers about six inches long, and made of thin metal. As I walked further along, I came across more … a lot more; they were scattered about everywhere.

I picked a few up with the idea of taking them home; perhaps I could fashion them into some kind of toy weapon to be used in our war games around the plantation. Then, as I made my way up over the sand dunes, I saw one sticking halfway out the sand. I pulled it out and found that it had a front bit attached to it. It looked exactly like a toy version of those large bombs they dropped from the old Lancaster bombers.

I got so excited that I set off back along the beach to show the others. All along the shore, I kept playing with it, throwing it up in the air and watching it come down like the bombs in the war movies.

When I arrived back at the spot where my mother and her companions were sitting, I was told they had all decided to return to one of the buses. I strolled over to where our bus was parked and stepped inside. At the rear of the bus sat a half dozen or so women chatting away amiably. I moved down the aisle towards them with my trophy and said, 'Look what I found, Ma!'

The unexpected outburst took me completely by surprise. The women got themselves into such a state. Legs flew up in the air. A variety of knee length pink bloomers flashed before my eyes; in fact, the whole back of the bus went into a complete state of panic.

My mother grabbed me and took me outside, and together we placed the object on the ground some distance from the bus. She immediately called my Dad who was at that moment standing with a group of men. He strolled over towards us wondering what all the commotion was. When my mother pointed to the object on the ground, he immediately let out an exclamation, like: *'Jesus Christ!'*

After the situation settled down and the appropriate method of disposal arranged, he took me aside and gave me a stern lecture on *Unexploded Bombs*. I was made to promise never to pick up anything that remotely resembled such a thing.

## The Local TA's Day at the Rifle Range

A week or so after arriving back to the safety of the Terrace, I told my pals about the incident and they were quite impressed. In fact, one of the older lads mentioned that we should take a wander up to see the military firing range, which was just past Helensfield. On certain weekends, the local TA do a few hours of target practice at the side of a narrow farm road leading to Gartmorn Dam.

The following Sunday, a bunch of us got together and decided to investigate. There was George from Kersegreen Road, Jackie Robertson from the Terrace, Andrew, John and a couple of lads from the newly built housing scheme called the Blackburns. We made our way towards the Public Park at the bottom of the Cattle Market, and down the road towards Patton and Baldwin's Woollen Mill, situated beside the banks of the Black Devon River. Even from that location, we could hear the sounds of rifle fire and the occasional short burst from a Bren-Gun.

At Helensfield, we turned right, making our way under the Alloa/Dunfermline railway-bridge near the Zetland Pit, and on up a narrow farm road passing the entrance of Hillend house. Thick bushes and trees ran along each side. The sounds of gunfire were quite loud now, and I must say I felt a wee bit apprehensive.

*We stood by enjoying a real military exercise...*

Then just round the next bend, parked on the narrow grass verge, stood a medium sized army truck, almost obscured among the thick bushes. Several soldiers were milling about, and I wondered if perhaps we weren't allowed to be here. A few of them turned and saw us approach. They appeared not to mind us, so we edged a little closer until we finished up standing a short distance from the firing line.

139

A number of soldiers were already preparing to move up to the firing point (a purpose built earthen platform on the banks of the roadside supported by a brick reinforced wall). Ground sheets were placed on the ground for the soldiers to lie on. As they lined up in front of their firing positions, their rifles by their sides, the duty sergeant snapped out an order. Without hesitation and in unison, they dropped onto their groundsheets and positioned their rifles at the ready. The sergeant snapped another command and they commenced firing.

Across the field, a couple of hundred yards ahead, I could see an elongated grass mound with a row of about half a dozen square targets. Then I noticed similar mounds further on, each spaced one hundred yards apart. They were used to test the various scales of accuracy, and to pick out the best individuals.

As we stood looking on, I got a wee bit curious regarding a small safety issue; for example, what if a farm worker were to cross in front of the firing line. When I mentioned it to one of the soldiers, he pointed to a flagpole on the far hill with a large red flag flying from it. That was a sign to anyone in the area that the rifle range is in use; also the sergeant and officer beside him kept a close look out.

We decided to wait about until the Bren-Guns had a go. Then after that, we thought of taking a look at Gartmorn Dam a short distance further along the road. Actually, the Bren-gun had some significance for our family in that—according to my mother—my Uncle, Francis Rogers from Musselburgh, engineered a small modification that set him up in business running his own engineering shop.

The gun itself was a Czechoslovakian lightweight quick firing machinegun; however, there apparently was a persistent jamming problem with the return mechanism. Uncle Francy, in some way, modified or invented a small swivel piece that regulated the return gases … Anyway, it was nice to know that there was a brain somewhere in the family.

As we stood by enjoying a front row view of this real live military exercise, it wasn't long before the Bren-Guns appeared and were soon made ready for use. There were two of them and as soon as their magazines were loaded and ready, the sergeant gave his command.

Hearing the sounds of real weapons going off and watching them from a position so close, was for me, a real treat; and the sound of rapid-fire machineguns were even more thrilling. I came away from there determined to become a soldier just as soon as I was old enough.

Before long, the soldiers broke for lunch, so we set off towards the dam. Gartmorn Dam is a beautiful man-made lake with a small island in the centre covered in trees. It was formed in the early eighteenth century, providing waterpower for the Alloa Coal Company's pumps. The source was near the village of Forest Mill where a channel or Lade diverts part of the Black Devon, cutting across the level contour of the land and flowing into the dam.

The Dam is a favourite spot for weekend visitors. Groups of walkers were already there, dressed in their Sunday best, and promenading up and down the embankment, occasionally stopping to feed the swans. Some had even brought their fishing rods. Apparently, the lake was full of pike and perch.

Sitting along the dam's embankment, looking at the clear water and watching the swans glide past, I began to fantasise about sailing out to the island, hoisting a black Jolly Roger flag, and burying our treasures in a secret spot somewhere in the middle. It would be some years later that I would get the chance to explore that island. It happened one winter during a very severe cold spell. The whole lake iced over thick enough to walk on. However, as we stepped onto the island, we had quite a bit of difficulty making our way into the interior due to the dense undergrowth. We soon gave up. At least our curiosity was satisfied.

Heading back down the small farm road towards home, we approached the firing range and found the soldiers had already packed up and left. While stopping to have a look around, one of our mates found a spent 303-cartridge shell. This set us all scouring the ground looking for more. I made my way around the front of the firing point and raked among the long grass. There were dozens scattered all over. Some were quite shiny, while others were a bit tarnished with lying about too long; still, they were quite a find.

As soon as I got home, I got out my mother's tin of Brasso and meticulously cleaned each one. They stood standing in a row on top of the Tallboy in my bedroom for months after.


## A Bus Enters Geordie Gray's Yard


As the last few days of our summer holiday were coming to an end, news got around of a recent addition to Geordie Gray's stock of wrecked vehicles. It was a big 1925 NS model double-decker bus … a double-decker bus with a difference. The whole vehicle was the colour of battleship-grey and painted on each side in very large print, the letters 'RN'. It was in fact, an ex-Royal Navy bus, most likely used for transporting naval personnel.

To us kids, it was like a magnet. We wasted no time in entering the yard to give it a good going-over. The bus already had all its seats taken out, and just above the driver's cabin, there was a large timber box. Its length was the same width as the bus and had a substantial looking lid with a latch to accommodate a padlock. We assumed it was used to carry guns and ammunition—our imaginations were a bit limited, especially where military objects were concerned.

In the months to come, this box would have for me yet another tale of near tragic results. But for now, the last remaining days of the holiday were spent playing in and around this interesting wreck. It was our new gang-hut and it had upstairs accommodation, a whole new concept in gang-hut design.

All too soon, the day arrived for the start of the new term. Our teacher was Miss Meekle, a tall bespectacled lady who wore her greying hair in a bun. The contrast between her and my previous teacher, Miss Hutcheson, was in her nature. Her character had a quality of natural calmness, but at the same time, still possessing that essential air of authority. She stood by the classroom door as we filed past. A couple of lassies had already brought her small posies of flowers for her desktop … how nice.

After arranging our seating—according to our academic skills—I settled into the usual tedious routine. My desk was situated at the top left end. From there, I could just make out through the east window, the large oak trees surrounding Clackmannan House. Over the next few months, in the course of my periodic daydreaming sessions, I would look out and observe the gradual and inexorable approach of winter.

# Chapter 10
# Crisis, Cubs and Poachers Locked in a Box

*"Aye! The nichts are fair drawin' in, Maggie,"* were some of the brief comments from the old folks as they passed each other in the street.

The evenings certainly were getting darker, and the air a bit crisper. The approaching cold weather usually meant digging out the warmer clothing, or Ma would deck us out with replacements from the Co-op Drapery department in the Main Street.

This particular year, I got a pair of woollen gloves, a Balaclava helmet, and a brand new pair of *tacketie-boots*. They were just ordinary army type boots with small steel tacks nailed on the soles, and a plate on the heel giving extra strength against wear and tear. Sometimes, for a bit of fun, I would scuff the tacks along the concrete footpaths creating great showers of sparks. When I think of it, those same boots may very well have been responsible for saving my life.

*The bus with a big coffin-like box above the driver's cabin…*

The incident occurred during a dark evening in late autumn. I arrived home from school at the usual time, and after our typical tea of egg and chips, I sat in the lounge room listening to the Children's Hour serial on the radio. As soon as it ended, I thought of paying a call on one of my pals.

John Patton lived in Balfour Street, he was quite a character; perhaps a bit eccentric—which was not that unusual, especially in our small community. A few days before, we bought ourselves battery torches and began venturing into dark mysterious places. On this occasion, we made our way down the footpath towards the Curling Pond, and entered Geordie Gray's yard.

Moving through the mass of wrecked vehicles was a bit of a hazard at the best of times, what with the assortment of old rusty car parts lying about the place; however, it all added to the challenge. John suggested we check out the old Ex-Royal Navy double-decker bus that had arrived in the yard a couple of months earlier. It was parked a bit further up the yard.

Now, there was a small problem with that. Although Geordie didn't mind kids playing down the end of the yard, he did warn us not to get too close to his workshop. From an adult's point of view, it was quite understandable: dangerous equipment, valuable tools etc. So, we moved cautiously towards the bus, making sure the beam from our lamps wouldn't be seen from Geordie's house further up; it could be construed as unlawful activity … which, I suppose it was … in a way.

There was one thing in our favour. Some time ago, Geordie had built himself a very large extension to his workshop just behind his house, and that gave us enough cover while playing in that particular spot.

As we approached the old bus, I began to feel a wee bit uneasy. Everything was so quiet with just the occasional sound of voices from somewhere amongst the glow of street lamps along Balfour and Castle Street; and the shape of this large object silhouetted in the darkness added to the creepy effect.

John made his way towards the rear and climbed up onto the platform. He then cautiously moved up the steps to the top deck, I followed close behind. We were only a minute or two up on the top deck when suddenly we both thought we heard something moving about outside. Immediately, we switched off our torches. After a minute or so, John made a sign, indicating that we should move to a better spot. Staying inside this bus would leave us with no means of escape.

As quietly as we could, we crept down the steps and into the yard. A few paces away from the bus, we stopped and crouched down, listening for the slightest sound. As the minutes passed, we began to think that maybe we had imagined the whole thing. Convincing ourselves that all was well, we continued rummaging about.

We moved towards the front of the vehicle and decided to check out the large wooden box mounted across the top of the driver's cabin. We climbed up and opened the great heavy lid. Both of us stepped inside and sat down at each end. It seemed a cosy little nook, and what a great hiding place. I thought perhaps, if we close the lid, it would make it that bit warmer … so I did. We sat inside the enclosed space, our torches giving the interior an atmosphere of a cosy nest.

After several minutes, we decided we'd had enough. I reached up to open the lid, but it appeared to be stuck. We both pushed with all our strength and still it wouldn't open. It didn't take us long to realise the seriousness of our situation. At the time, we had no idea what was causing the lid to jam. Apparently, the latch on the lid had slipped over the padlock ring on the outside of the box locking us in.

Within the next few seconds, deep concern was fast giving way to a state of complete panic. We started beating on the side of the box and shouting as loud as we could for help. I didn't want to admit that all our shouting and screaming was actually quite useless; we must be at least a hundred yards from any public place, and who would be wandering about this place in the dark.

We sat in that confined spot, barely looking at each other, because the sight of our faces had disaster written all over them. There was no conversation between us, we just cried and sobbed continually, occasionally shouting futile cries for help. I had not even given a thought as to how long it would be before anyone would be able to find us. I began thinking of options … perhaps Mr Gray would be able to hear our cries in the morning. The realisation of that thought suddenly sent me into a state of deep depression. The prospect of spending one night in this box was too awful to contemplate, and as it was the beginning of the week, there would be no kids around until the weekend. Moreover, what if our cries for help could not be heard due to the thickness of this God-awful box— what then? We may be in here for days … weeks … forever!

I got so worked up that I started shouting at the pitch of my voice and kicked wildly at the lid with my new boots. Both of us gave what seemed our very last effort at something. Suddenly, after about the third or fourth bash on the lid, it flipped open; but it was just for a second, it dropped back down and slammed shut again.

John and I stopped and looked at each other. The expression of hope in our faces and the prospect of a solution to our dilemma gave us both an overwhelming sense of purpose. He said in a quiet voice, 'Do that again. Only this time I'll put some pressure on the lid with my feet.' I began kicking as hard as I could, then suddenly, after about the third kick, the lid sprung open and the fresh evening air greeted us with an almost indifferent sigh of relief.

As we rose to our feet, taking in a few breaths of the evening air, we suddenly heard a sound. It was the sound of someone whistling a tune. At first, we couldn't make out anything through the darkness. Just then, we saw a man standing near the wall at the end of Dukestreet. He was obviously out for an evening walk. Most likely, this was who we heard moving about earlier. John shouted across to him something like: 'You old bastard! Didn't you hear our cries for help?' … There was no reply.

On the way home, John and I parted at the top of the Terrace. We had certainly experienced a whole new perspective on life. I walked on towards my home, opened the back door and stepped inside to be confronted with the scene of my mother and my two brothers arguing over a piece of toast and cheese. My tragic tale of near catastrophic proportions passed without much interest. The issue over the choice of supper was far more urgent.

A year or so later, John left the district to join other family members in America. I did receive two or three letters from his new home in Cleveland, Ohio, and I sent him one or two, but after a time, the letters stopped coming and we gradually lost touch. The memory of that incident would never leave me, and every now and then, I wonder if old John, wherever he is, still remembers that time.

## Joining the Cubs

Over the next couple of weeks, things settled down and the realisation of what could have happened, with its tragic consequences, soon passed. A few weeks later, I got involved with the local Wolf Cubs.

One evening after school, I stood under the electric streetlamp at the end of the Terrace with a few pals discussing the approach of Halloween and Guy Fox night. Moments later, we saw Stewart Hill coming out of his place and walking towards us. He was heading off to his Cubs night, and all dressed up in the group's uniform: a green schoolboy type cap with yellow trimmings, and the red neck scarf.

Under his coat, I noticed he had quite a few round and oval shaped badges sewn to his jersey. He called them merit badges, and to win them, you had to perform certain tasks, like an ability, or skill in something: athletics, artwork, or any useful project. My curiosity slightly stirred, I wanted to know more, so some of us decided to accompany him down to the meeting hall.

The Cubs conducted their activities on Friday evenings down at the Public School Drill Hall, and immediately after the Cub's session, the Boy Scouts turned up for their meeting. When we arrived at the main gate of the school, we met up with two or three other lads hanging around waiting for the man in charge; his name was Bert Gillespie. Bert was a man in his mid-twenties with quite a pleasing disposition. He had a quality that was ideally suited for dealing with young lads. I thought it was a pity that some of our teachers were not more like him.

We hadn't waited long before the rest of the pack showed up, followed by the man himself. It seemed strange entering the school area in the evening when normally I couldn't wait to get out of it. As we stepped inside the drill hall, we were introduced to Bert, and of course, we knew most of the other lads; a few of them were my classmates.

The first thing we all had to go through before the start of the evening's activities was this very odd ritual. To me, it seemed just a wee bit on the weird side. For example, Bert produced a long pole with the figure of a wolf's head stuck on top. He then uttered a few strange esoteric chants. The regular lads scrambled around him shouting something like: *"We'll dib, dib, dob, etc, etc, etc. ..."* I never could come to terms with that sort of thing, and actually, when the occasion arose at each meeting, I just silently mimed the whole thing.

Nevertheless, the whole experience was generally quite good fun, and we attended the sessions every Friday.

Eventually, Ma bought us the appropriate cap and scarf. In a few weeks, I had received my first badge. It was the wolf badge, and this was awarded for reciting the *Cubs Sacred Oath* … I stuffed it up quite a bit; however, they gave me the badge anyway.

During all this, my young brother Andrew was getting along just like the rest of us, until the evening of the Cubs Halloween party where he ended up getting himself cashiered … drummed out of the Cubs in disgrace.

The incident occurred as the party was about to end. Up until then, everything was rolling along quite well with the usual sticky-bun competition, and pinning the tail on the old donkey. All that remained now was the ducking for apples in the large basin of water; they were actually our own apples, we each brought one along especially for this event.

Anyway, there they were, floating about in the big basin in the middle of the hall, and it was looking suspiciously like the evening's activities were drawing to a close. While Bert stood centre stage, going through, what seemed to us, his wind-up address, we began looking sideways at each other as if to say: *"Hello, hello …"*

It looked as if our apples were going to be left to the organisers as a nice little take-home bonus; some of us were of the opinion that this should not be allowed to happen. Suddenly, there was a mad scramble and Cubs of all shapes and sizes surrounded the basin. I looked about and thought, if I don't get in there quick, I'm going to be left with nothing. I made a headlong charge straight through someone's legs and just managed to grab one of the apples. I immediately struggled free and popped it in my jacket pocket. Meanwhile, Mr Gillespie was franticly trying to maintain a bit of order.

Eventually, things settled down. The basin sat on the floor, empty of everything except a bit of water swishing gently back and forth on the bottom. Bert was furious, he ranted on about the disgraceful conduct of our actions, and that we should never forget the Cub's golden rules, and what it meant to live up to those ideals—of course, it all went over our heads.

The boys who started the whole debacle were immediately singled out to be harshly reprimanded, and the chief instigators were told, right there and then, to leave the hall and never return … my young brother was one of them.

Now, to think that he was devastated by the whole affair, or that he suffered any remorse would be quite wrong. He thought the whole incident very amusing. His mischievous outgoing personality and his cheeky sense of humour appeared to see right through life's little absurdities.

# Changes: Some Good, Some Not So

Bonfire night was once again upon us, and stepping out with a few pals to see who had the biggest pile of logs and scrap timber ready for the first strike of the matchstick was always an exciting time. As for the fireworks side of things, there were never any great displays, perhaps because no one thought the occasion worthy of such extravagance, like the end of a war, or the beginning of a new millennium. We were happy enough with our small paper bag full of bangers, cartwheels and rockets—most of them used up days before the actual event.

For me, the bonfires on Guy Fox night were becoming a little bit of an anti-climax. The exciting bit was at the very start. As soon as we set the stack of timber alight, there was the initial exhilaration of raging flames and showers of exploding sparks; but all too soon, after the fire reached its peak, it descended into a quiet wavering glow. Some of us would then get together and head off to visit other bonfire sights around town.

The Blackburns: a recently built housing scheme along Balfour St (now renamed Lochies Rd) was our first port of call. An interesting arrangement of houses built in the shape of a square with a children's playpen situated in the centre. It was in this area that the new residents decided to have their first bonfire night.

As we approached, we could see the glow of the flames above the rooftops. Pedestrian walkways between the house-blocks gave access to the playpen. We already knew most of the Blackburn kids as there were quite a number from the now vacant houses at The Green and Dukestreet. The rest of the families had moved into the other new housing scheme down at The Pottery.

Although all the residents of The Green and Dukestreet were highly delighted to move out of those old eighteenth century miner's cottages and into a more modern accommodation, it left the Gang in a very sad state. The boys of the Terrace were all that was left to cope with the now superior ranks of the Zetland Street boys. Eventually, we had to concede to an undeclared peace.

But, a short while before that, there was quite an amusing incident during one of our last confrontations. It occurred just round the corner near old Haerie's place. A number of lads from Zetland Street were playing in the ruins of The Green when most of us from the Terrace turned up. We all started taunting each other, and moments later, Pat Flynn, one of the oldest in our group, stepped forward and began picking on one of the lads, saying something like: 'Go on, hit me here …' (pointing to his chin). During this course of goading, wee Geordie Solomon manoeuvred himself behind Pat and whacked him on the bum with a stick. Suddenly, Pat fell to the ground in agony and had to be carried away. We were all very surprised and taken aback. Pat was about twice the size of wee Geordie, and the blow to his rear couldn't have been that serious … Pat's younger brother, Tommy, later explained … It seemed he had quite a large boil on his backside, and Wee Geordie hit it right on the spot. Everyone fell into fits of laughter.

The next few weeks gradually took on preparations for the Christmas festivities, and the celebrations for the end of another year. A special event was planned up at Linn Mill and our school would be playing a part—or I should say, the lads from St Mungo's school in Alloa, using the woodwork facilities in our school drill hall.

The project was to illuminate the waterfalls at Linn Mill, and also using the old mill shed as a viewing area and restaurant. The lads from St Mungo's were given the task of building a large-scale model of the Clackmannan tower. The result was a beautiful replica of the tower standing about four feet in height. It was then placed out on one of the rocks at the bottom of the falls.

Although I never actual saw the evening display with all the bright lights, I did manage to visit the scene during the day … it looked quite impressive.

Also, around this time, I started noticing some real changes. Our Christmas gifts increased in number and sophistication: tin soldiers with realistic coloured uniforms, toy castles with working drawbridges, and heaps of board games—and not only were our stockings overflowing with all sorts of sweets and chocolates, there were also various packets and boxes of confectionary spread out all over the room. The deprivations of post-war Britain had finally ended.

By the end of the week, a new year would begin; a year so full of new beginnings and changes that it seemed someone, or something had come along, lifted up the old grey curtain, and finally let in the light. The year 1953 was a year like no other—well, for me anyway. For starters, I will be one decade old on my birthday—a two-digit number!

Apart from that significant fact, a number of other happenings gave the year a feeling that this was the dawning of a new era: the crowning of the Queen at Westminster; Edmund Hillary and Tenzing Norgay were the first people to climb the highest mountain on earth; Briton's involvement in the Korean War ended, and Joe Stalin finally died.

Closer to home, Alloa hosts the Highland Show down at the park beside the tower. For me, the highlight of the event was the display given by the Canadian Mounted Police. In addition to that, and due to the spectacular event, I witnessed another unfamiliar sight. Our town actually experienced something that only happened in major cities and only during certain times of the day—a traffic jam. We stood on the school's perimeter wall looking out onto a scene of cars stretching bumper to bumper all the way along the main road. I think, even to this day, there has never been anything like it, and most likely never will be again due to the by-pass.

Another titbit of local news was that auld Haerie Ferguson, the baker at the end of Castle Street, started a new enterprise. He bought himself a fish and chip van and parked it along the edge of Balfour Street (Lochies Rd) in the vacant piece of ground across our back garden fence. For us, it was very handy. Just a hop over our back fence, and within minutes, I was back home with all our fish suppers. But, later that year, a tragic event would put an end to his new venture.

One evening, while standing in a small group waiting for my thrupenny bag, I noticed that the old man was not quite himself. He seemed a bit confused about things, and moments later, something had caught alight around the deep fryer. He tried to pat the flames out with a cloth, but it all got a bit too much for him. Within minutes, the flames got out of control and the whole interior was soon well and truly ablaze. Someone called in the Alloa fire brigade, but by the time they arrived, Haerie's chipper was just a smouldering heap. Not long after that, the old man past away.

## The Poachers' Loss

The year 1953 seemed to be a mixture of highlights and tragedies. Devastating floods hit the east coast of England killing several hundred people, and on January of that year, a car ferry from Stranraer sank in the Irish Sea during one of the worst gales in living memory, claiming the lives of more than 130 passengers and crew. The captain apparently went down with his ship.

But, the greatest tragedy, as far as I was concerned, was a contagion called myxomatosis; a virulent infection that almost wiped out the whole rabbit population. I suppose it could be described as the *Bunnies Black Death*. The thought that never again would we see bunny rabbits hopping about the fields left me with a feeling of loss. The harvest time activity of walking behind the wheat binders with our cudgels, and the taste of Ma's delicious rabbit pies would soon be a thing of the past.

Then sadly, there's the local poachers. I imagine they wouldn't be too pleased about the situation; although, they still had the ducks, pheasants and woodpigeons.

Now and then we would come across a known poacher emerging from the private estates, his coat bulging with the days catch, and his gun cleverly concealed (usually a small *four-ten* shot gun. The larger twelve-gauge took a bit more of an effort to hide among the clothing).

However, not all gun owners were poachers. Some were properly licensed, and had the appropriate permits for particular hunting areas. The banks of the River Forth were a popular spot with a variety of duck and quail. The woodlands were another favourite place, mainly for Woodpigeons. Quite often, while playing in the Back Wood down at The Pottery, we would hear the sound of gunfire coming from somewhere among the trees. Then, every now and then, we would come across a poacher's hide. This was always considered a rare discovery. Generally, they were cleverly hidden in hedgerows or among the dense bushes.

The method of construction was mainly thin branches tied together and covered with grassy material to give maximum camouflage, with just a small opening looking out over the target area. They were so well hidden that actually finding one was usually by chance, and on those rare occasions, our childish imaginations took over. A secret hideout; a place where only trusted gang members would be invited. To a child's mind, having a secret was like possessing something of great value. Your particular little gang of brothers knew something that others did not.

On one occasion, we happened to come across one in a very unusual place. Chances of ever finding it, even by accident, would have been at least a thousand to one.

One weekend, after playing in the Back Wood, we decided to take a brake under the trees. Some of us took the opportunity to emulate the grown-ups by having a pretend smoke on our sweetie cigarettes, while others lit up a cinnamon stick, a cigarette paper rolled round it to give it that authentic touch.

In the course of our activities, we found ourselves in an unfamiliar part of the wood; even the trees seemed a bit closer together, giving the immediate surroundings a slightly darker ambiance.

While we sat down on the soft pine needles with our backs against the trees, an object suddenly dropped from above and landed among us. We immediately recognised it. It was a spent shotgun cartridge. We began looking about wondering if somebody was playing tricks on us by hiding behind the trees and throwing things at us. After a brief search of the vicinity, we were sure there was no one else about. But, where did it come from?

We looked up above us and could see no reason for such a thing being up in the trees. Then, one of our gang thought he saw something. The branches seemed particularly thick around the top of one of the trees. He decided to investigate. While he struggled up the dense scratchy branches, we sat around the bottom and waited. Some of us thought he was being a bit too idiotic. Several minutes later, he shouted from the top: 'Hey! Look what I've found!'

That remark, of course, triggered our curiosity. After quite an effort, we reached the spot. It was a platform made of small branches and secured with pieces of cord. Someone had obviously gone to extraordinary lengths. The size of it was just big enough to accommodate one adult, or two of us, so we took turns in climbing onto it.

It was a strange experience. I felt I had entered another world. It was like suddenly stepping into the daylight, and the scene of the woodland canopy stretching out before me instantly stirred my imagination. To me, it looked like the mysterious world of the treetop people in the Rupert Bear stories.

But, there was something about the spot that made me a bit curious. If the whole idea of the platform was to bag a few woodpigeons, how would the poacher collect his catch? It was absurd to think that each time he bagged something, he would then climb down the tree, pick up the catch and climb back up. The only solution I could think of was that he must have an accomplice waiting on the ground … very confusing.

## Getting to Know Mr Chalmers

Sometime later, Stewart Hill's older brother Wullie and I got involved with doing some chores for old Mr Chalmers, the pigeon fancier at the end of Dukestreet—who, we suspected, did a bit of poaching in his time. He certainly had all the necessary kit: a Twelve-Gauge, a small Four-Ten, and a large single barrel Goose-Gun; he even kept a couple of ferrets.

We did things like, feed the hens, collect the eggs, and clean out his pigeon loft down at his allotment. In return, we could help ourselves to as many bantam eggs as were produced. There weren't that many, and only half the size of hens' eggs; still, we enjoyed the feeling of doing something useful.

This association with the old man actually began over a very shameful incident. In fact, several weeks before we got involved with him, things between us were very awkward. Even PC Kettles was called in.

It all started while playing down at Geordie Gray's yard. I had briefly left the group to go fossicking for bits of timber for the campfire. I approached the end of old Chalmers' allotment and discovered that a few of his hens had escaped through a gap in the hedge. I strolled up to them to have a closer look; and then I thought I would reach down and pat one on the head like a pet. Suddenly, there was a bit of fluttering and squawking, and one of the hens pecked me on the hand. It gave me quite a sting. A small globule of blood formed around the spot. I was so taken aback by the shear aggressiveness from such a small creature that I ran as fast as I could back to the others and told them what happened.

Without further ado, Wullie Hill took charge and immediately formed a posse. We set off with the purpose of apprehending the culprit.

The identification parade that took place was, to say the least, a bit unfair; in other words, you could say the whole scene was conducted in the spirit of *lynch-mob mentality*. 'OK,' said Wullie, determined to see justice carried out, 'Which one was it?'

Carried along by the hysteria of the moment, I pointed to one particular creature—although they all looked alike. A short struggle ensued, followed by much shouting and squawking. After apprehending the poor unfortunate hen, we marched back to the campfire and immediately held a trial. One of us was assigned the duty of holding onto the small pathetic looking prisoner while sentence was passed. That poor defenceless creature was found guilty and immediately strung up by the neck until it expired.

Several minutes later, when the frenzy of activity abated, some of us started having deep feelings of regret. The fun element in our general activity deteriorated rapidly. Soon, we began drifting off in random groups along the footpath towards home. As for the hen; it was left hanging on the end of the string.

A day or so after, PC Kettles knocked on our front door. Apparently, some of the younger kids had told old Mr Chambers about the incident, who in turn, called the police. Fortunately, the matter was not taken any further. There was some sort of arrangement between our parents and Mr Chalmers in the way of compensation.

Nevertheless, the childish cruelty of that incident haunted me for some time.

Weeks passed, and it was only a thought that maybe Wullie and I should go down to see old Mr Chalmers to apologise in person. I was a bit apprehensive at first, but Wullie seemed more determined. I followed him down towards the end of Dukestreet and we entered the allotment. Mr Chalmers was sitting up on the landing of his pigeon loft. He looked down at us, but said nothing.

I stood a couple of paces behind Wullie. It was a very awkward moment … no one was saying anything. Wullie slowly approached the bottom of the steel ladder leading up to the landing … still nothing was said. Then he climbed up a couple of rungs and uttered something like: 'Eh … we're awfie sorry Mr Chalmers … aboot the hen …' The old man turned his head and eyed the two of us briefly, then resumed his silent posture, his attention focused on his flock of pigeons circling above.

Wullie took another step up and to my surprise, began discussing the finer points of racing pigeons. 'Is that what they call a blue-bar?' pointing to one that had just landed on the roof of the loft. 'No,' said old Chalmers, 'that's a blue-checker.' He went on in a casual tone, pointing out the other types. Before long, we were all sitting side-by-side on the landing, the tense atmosphere dissolving by the minute.

Shortly after, the old man showed us around his yard. First, he took us to the spot near the gate where he kept the feed for the livestock. Two 45-gallon drums, one containing grain for the hens, and the other, beans for the pigeons. He took the lid off one and reached in, scooping out a small bowl of wheat. We entered the hen-run, which took up about a third of the yard. A high wire-mesh fence kept the birds from wandering around his small area of garden. Part of the pen was used to hold the half dozen or so bantams.

Feeding the hens and collecting the new laid eggs was great fun. The small wooden hen house had rows of nesting boxes along one side, and several spars where they would spend their nights perched along them. The rest of the yard was used to grow all sorts of vegetables. Down one side, he had rows of potatoes and brussels sprouts. The middle section had rows of gooseberries, blackcurrants, raspberries and strawberries. Every now and then, he would harvest a few vegetables and berries, and after loading up the basket on his bicycle, he headed off to his home in Dundas Crescent.

As the weeks past, Wullie and I took on the basic tasks of cleaning out the loft, feeding the livestock, including the two ferrets. We were warned to be extra careful when feeding the ferrets; apparently, they were apt to bite. Then of course, there were his two gun dogs; a pair of black cocker spaniels. I felt a bit sorry for them being locked up all day under the pigeon loft. Although their area was quite spacious, it still didn't seem right. I elected to take them out occasionally for a bit of exercise, just around the field between his yard and the plantation. Sometimes, we even took the pigeons out for a bit of exercise.

Mr Chalmers would select a half dozen or so of his best racers and put them into a special basket. We were then given enough money for the return fare to Kincardine. Once arriving there, we made for the bridge that crossed the River Forth. As soon as we arrived at the middle, we opened the basket and watched them fly off, taking note of the time.

Meanwhile, Mr Chalmers, waiting back at the loft, could judge which would be the best ones to send off to the big national races. There was the local event over at Locharby, and the major one at Rennes in France. For that occasion, the great basket was brought out, and the chosen birds placed inside, each fitted with a uniquely numbered rubber ring around one leg. All the baskets from different competitors were then sent off by rail and across the Channel to the starting point in West France.

A day after the scheduled release and start of the race, we stood by the loft with binoculars scouring the horizon looking for any sign of them. Mr Chalmers sat in his chair on the veranda and waited, the special timing-clock close by his side. The drill was, as soon as the first one arrived and coaxed into the loft, the other race would then commence. Grabbing hold of the bird as quickly as possible and removing the rubber ring from its leg. The ring was then put in a small capsule and then into the clock. A handle was then turned on the side of the clock locking the capsule inside and recording the time. The clocks were then sent off to the judges who took note of the time and the number on the rubber ring.

Unfortunately, on that one particular occasion, we were not successful, but the fun and excitement of being involved in an international competition was great, and just seeing the birds arrive from such a long way off, was for me, an incredible feat.

Those days spent down at old Mr Chalmers' yard were magical. The sense of purpose and being involved in interesting projects, like the time he arrived with a couple of dozen newly hatched chickens and raised them in a large specially adapted box with an oil lamp in the centre to maintain the correct temperature. Watching them grow from wee yellow coloured fluffy balls to long legged pullets was an interesting spectacle.

The old man even showed me the correct way to use a catapult, or *Guttie*, as we called it. After a few weeks of practice, I got quite good at hitting empty tin cans off the wall. It got to the stage where Wullie and I felt we were part owners of the place.

However, several months passed by and we began to notice that the old man's visits to the yard were getting less and less. Sometimes we wouldn't see him for the whole week.

Eventually, his daughter, Mrs Bennet with her son Michael, arrived at the yard and told us the place was going to be sold due to Mr Chalmers' health. We helped as much as we could, but with the old man no longer around, the place began to lose something. Eventually, Wullie and I drifted off. We never did hear what became of Mr Chalmers. I assume he passed away shortly after.

# Chapter 11
# Coronation Year

Even though most of the folks in our community appeared—to say the least—a bit indifferent regarding the British Royal family, there was however, an atmosphere of general excitement at the approach of Princess Elizabeth's coronation, especially among all the kids. The historic event scheduled to take place in July had all the trappings of an extra special occasion. Large mugs embossed with the Royal Coat of Arms, and pictures of the new Queen and the Duke of Edinburgh (Prince Philip) were handed out to every child in the country. Television sales soared due to the announcement that the whole event would be televised. John, Andrew and I pestered our folks to get one, but it was not to be; at least, not for a few more months. They told us that as our holiday plans meant we would be away from home during the whole event, it would be pointless to get one at this time.

Apparently, our holiday was arranged to fit in with Dad's union business. On that particular year, the National Union of Mineworkers annual conference was to be held up in Aberdeen, and Dad, being an active union delegate, was selected to attend.

Our headmaster, Mr Johnston, gave us special permission to have that particular week off from school. At least, it was a break from our usual visit to the relatives over in the Lothians, especially since we would be meeting up with most of them later in the year at the annual Scottish Miners' Gala day (an event first organised in 1947 to celebrate the winning of the five-day working week).

On Monday, the 1st of June, we made an early start and caught the local bus to Stirling. At the main bus station in Stirling, we hung about waiting for our connection to take us all the way to Aberdeen. I had travelled east to the Lothians and west to Glasgow and Coatbridge to visit relatives, but I had never ventured this far North before ... Aberdeen, the *Granite City* with its *Northern Lights*.

When my mother first mentioned the term, *Northern Lights*, I expected something like the illuminations at Blackpool. I had never heard of the term, *Aurora Borealis* before, and probably wouldn't have got my tongue around the word let alone know what it meant. Anyway, it was the wrong time of the year for it.

Half an hour or so later, a large forty-five-seated bus pulled into the station with *Aberdeen* displayed in the top window. After loading the cases into the bus's rear luggage compartment, we were on our way. I sat for a while looking out at the passing landscape until eventually I got a bit bored. I think I dozed off a couple of times. Then someone on the bus mentioned a notorious spot just south of Aberdeen called, *The Devil's Elbow*, a treacherous bend in the road that earned itself a reputation for causing serious accidents.

When we approached the place, the driver slowed down and sure enough, the bend seemed to turn in on itself with quite a steep drop on the outer edge. It didn't take much imagination to see why it earned the name … a foggy night … a bit of black ice, and the chances of a mishap would most likely be odds-on.

We arrived at Bell's Hotel in George Street just in time for tea. After settling into our room, we made our way downstairs to the first floor and waited in the lounge. Moments later, a waitress appeared and began sounding a small gong by the doorway. My brothers and I were very impressed. Being summoned to tea in such a manner belonged to the world of the gentry, to the characters in the novels of P. G. Wodehouse and Agatha Christie, not for the likes of us—we didn't know that that was the norm in most hotels.

About a day or so later, we persuaded the waitress to let us have a go at sounding the gong before each meal. It helped break up the boredom of sitting around the lounge, trying to maintain a degree of quiet self-control so as not to upset the other guests.

That week in Aberdeen was not the most exciting holiday I'd ever had. The weather was—to say the least—abysmal, and as Dad was out most days attending the NUM conference, we just hung about in the hotel lounge playing endless games of cards and dominoes. It wasn't much fun for Ma either. She would get us all dressed up to wander the streets looking into shop windows.

One evening we did manage to see a movie at the picture house just around the corner: *The Desert Rats,* with the Australian actor, Chips Rafferty. Then, the day before returning home, Dad had the rest of the time off. We got on a bus and ventured out to the seaside … It was deserted. The wind and grains of sand flew about in all directions, sporadic bursts of drizzling rain rattled across the beach. We had to take refuge in a bus shelter … so, it was back to the hotel.

## The Book Prize Shock

On returning to school, classroom activities, before the start of the long summer break, included rehearsing some chorus singing for the end-of-term concert. On that day, just after our stage performances, there would be the handing out of the book prizes to those who achieved certain scholarly top marks.

When the headmaster passed the list of our class prize-winners to Miss Meekle, she immediately read them out to the class. At the top of the list were the usual bright-sparks; but … then came the shocker! My name was called out! The teacher announced that this year there was to be a special prize for handwork! It looked as if the whole class went into a state of suspended shock. All I remember seeing at that moment was the sea of open mouthed faces staring at me.

During that term in Miss Meekle's class, we were given needlework projects. My particular choice from the list was a sort of carrier bag. The set of instructions were not that difficult to follow. With different lengths of coloured wool, I stitched a type of floral design into the face side, and also a pattern around the edges with red wool. I must say, I was quite pleased with the result. My mother actually used it for quite a number of years after. Being awarded a prize was certainly quite a boost to my confidence.

The prize-book was Dean Swift's, *Gulliver's Travels*. However, the pleasurable feeling of the first announcement gave way to the trauma of waiting for my name to be called out on the prize-giving day. The whole school assembled up at the town hall. After each class gave its short pre-rehearsed performance (usually a group song and a bit of a dance from the girls) the stage was then set for the finale. The table full of books sat centre-stage with the teachers seated around up-stage. The headmaster then began announcing the first lot of prize-winners.

I sat through the whole event in a state of nervous anticipation. My pals, giving me the occasional nudge and a wink, did not help the situation one little bit. The sound of my name came like a thump, and without being conscious of how I managed to arrive at the table, I found myself taking the book with one hand and shaking the headmaster's with the other. The applause and cheers from my classmates—with that little extra enthusiasm for an underdog—rang in my ears as I made my way back to my seat.

After the windup of the presentations, the headmaster made an announcement, saying that after the summer break, the school would be hosting an exchange teacher from the United States, and that Miss Kennedy—our next term teacher—would be swapping places as the guest teacher of an American school.

This was exciting stuff. We all began speculating about what this teacher was going to be like. Would it be a man or a woman? Our anticipation was like looking forward to meeting some celebrity. Meanwhile, we had the next few weeks of serious playing, and doing the usual summer holiday things.

## The Edinburgh Gala Day

The proceedings began up in the old part of Edinburgh with the grand parade down the High Street towards Holyrood Park. Pipe-bands lead the procession of the various coalfield branches, each carrying their own particular banner, and following directly behind them, the members of their families. It was reported that the year 1953, had a record crowd of nearly 100,000.

Personally, I found the whole event a bit over-whelming. However, there was one interesting scene involving a well-known celebrity. Both Andrew and I sat on the grass near the podium and listened to the union secretary, Abe Moffat, introduce the famous Labour MP, Aneurin Bevan. We were very impressed with the way Mr Bevan spoke; he was animated and passionate. However, the subject matter was a little over our heads.

The issues concerning the plight of the working people seemed an admirable cause, and most union demands seemed right and proper—at the time. However, like all just causes, the practical bits tend to get a bit lost among the ambitious and the feeble-minded. The farcical situation portrayed by that excellent film, *I'm All Right Jack,* with Peter Sellers playing the role of the union delegate, gave an account of how the real injustices got lost amongst some workers trivial demands. I often overheard my Dad and his comrades object to some of the pitiful reasons for going out on strike.

However, the day was not all politics. There were the competitions just like our local Gala day; but somehow, I wasn't that keen to enter them. The whole event seemed so big, and it just didn't seem the same as racing against our pals back home.

Ma and Dad gave instructions on how to find each other in the event that we got lost among the huge crowd. I joined some of my cousins in an attempt to walk up the top of Arthur's Seat Hill, but I changed my mind quarter way up and returned to chase Ma and Dad for more money to buy yet more ice cream and sweets.

When I got to the chosen spot, I found the mothers there. Dad and the rest of the men were lost somewhere in the midst of the great beer tent. Eventually, the day wound up with a quick visit to Grandma and Grandpa Stanton's place in Musselburgh, and then back home on that long tedious journey by bus.

## Rafting on the Black Devon

During a warm lazy day, around the first week of our holiday, a group of us got together and decided on a bit of a paddle at one of our favourite swimming spots: the *Dookin-Hole* down at the bottom of the Riccarton. After a while we noticed a couple of lads across on the other side of the river. They told us they were making their way further downstream towards the Mary Bridge; apparently, some of the boys from The Pottery had built a raft and they were off to find out if they could have a go on it.

We immediately got out of the water and decided to investigate. After drying ourselves off, we hurriedly put on our cloths and made our way across the bridge and into the field on the North bank of the river. This was the quickest way to follow the river, as the Woollen Mill, situated on the South bank, meant a detour around the public park.

We crossed the small burn that ran from the Zetland colliery, and hacked our way through the scrubby bushes surrounding the old quarry. After crossing over the banks of the Alloa and Kincardine railway line, and just a short distance further along, we heard the yells and shouts from the lads standing around the banks.

As soon as we arrived at the spot, we saw Bobby Airnes (one of the older lads, who we knew from The Green and was now living in one of the recently built houses in Kersegreen Road), standing on a raft made of small tree trunks tied together. He looked as if he was struggling to keep his balance, and the water swished over the deck wetting the soles of his feet. It was all very disappointing.

I had imagined something much more practical where you could stroll about the deck in reasonable comfort without the fear of capsizing. This raft, although quite big, was very awkward and apparently difficult to manoeuvre. Bobby had to stand close to the centre to achieve maximum stability.

His brother Billy arrived shortly after with another log and they squeezed it in with the rest of the timbers. There was a slight improvement, but it still lacked that stability. I could see that my early sketches of the raft I intended to build would need a lot of thought.

The problem would be solved several years later while on a walk with my Dad down at the Alloa docks. Moored in the small harbour was this medium sized ship from the Baltic region. A sailor was doing some work on the side of it near the water line. He stood on a small raft tied to the side of the boat. It was quite a simple construction, consisting of two large forty-five gallon drums, and some timber tied to it. The deck of this small raft stood well out of the water and seemed quite stable. This gave me the idea.

I began by using four empty five-gallon drums; a common item found strewn about the old quarry on the opposite bank of the Woollen Mill, now being used as a tip. There was also plenty of scrap timber, especially old floorboards. I placed the square drums in position and laid the flooring over them; however, my method of securing the timbers to the drums would end in disaster on the maiden voyage … I used nails.

When I completed the construction, I launched it into the Mill Weir at the deepest part of the river—it worked! I sat on the deck and paddled out to the middle. The water line was a good six or eight inches below the deck surface. I was overcome with excitement. I paddled up and down that small stretch of the river while some of the Mill employees looked out from the windows above and cheered.

Then I noticed that the raft was getting a bit low in the water. The front end was tipping up and the back dipped. I clung onto the front drums and kicked my way back to the bank. I just managed to grab hold of a branch from an overhanging bush and pulled myself up. Several of the Mill lassies thought the whole incident very funny, their laughter echoed along the length of the river.

The problem was, securing the timbers to the drums with nails. I thought that because the raft would be far enough out of the water, there would be no problem; however, the splashing about with the paddle and the bobbing up and down, gradually allowed a bit of water in through the small nail holes. So, it was back to the drawing board.

But, this idea had potential. With the help from two of my pals, Dennis McKean and Jim McMillan, we solved the problem by building the deck with a rim nailed around the edges, holding the drums in place. After the test voyage up and down the Mill Weir, we decided that we should transport the raft to a better location. In addition, we should increase the size to accommodate the three of us.

The Fairlies: a stretch of the Black Devon River about a couple of hundred yards upstream from Linn Mill was an ideal spot. The river depth was a constant four or five feet and ran a good mile or so without rapids or dangerous protruding obstacles. We could have hours of fun and adventure paddling up and down the whole length.

Unfortunately, there was a small problem regarding transport. We could only move so much at a time, and after a couple of laborious trips, first with the drums and then the pieces of timber, we put the whole exercise on hold to be completed at some later date. Sadly, that other time never arrived, and half the raft is probably still lying somewhere on the banks of the Fairlies.

My long held ambition to emulate the adventures of Tom Sawyer and Huck Finn gradually faded with time. It was left up to my older brother John and his pal Jack Adamson from Woodside Terrace some years later. They built themselves a timber-framed canvas covered canoe, coated the whole thing with tar and took it down the Black Devon passed the Craigrie. It was a tremendous success. Of course, the main difference was, they had left school and were earning a weekly wage; purchasing the right materials was no longer a problem.

## The Cousin Out of Africa

One day during the summer break, Ma informed us that we were having visitors: Aunty Mashie, Uncle Fred and Cousin Norman. This was, for us, a particularly exotic branch of the family.

Just before the war, my Aunt and Uncle moved down to Bedfordshire in England. Mashie worked for Reuters News, and Uncle Fred was an electrical engineer. Then soon after the war, they immigrated to Kenya, East Africa. Every now and then, we would hear interesting accounts of their experiences from that part of the world, like Cousin Norman out hunting lions with his .22 rifle; their house full of native servants; and how they coped with the threat from the Mau Mau terrorists.

On the day they arrived, the first thing that caught my attention was the sound of their car pulling up in front of our house—it was a very impressive looking model, something like a Wolseley or Humber; anyway, it certainly caught the eye from some of our neighbours.

As I stood watching them step out of the vehicle, I was suddenly confronted by an interesting sight. It was Cousin Norman dressed in a short sleeve safari suit, and wearing a wide brim bush hat with a thin leopard skin band. He looked like a character straight out of an Ernest Hemingway novel; the image of a young white hunter.

My mother immediately opened the front door to greet them. As we all settled ourselves down with a cup of tea, I sat about on the carpet listening to the general conversation. I was particularly taken with the tone of my cousin's voice. It was definitely not Scottish, not even regional English, more neutral, like the sound of a lad from a *Billy Bunter* boarding school.

For as young as I was, I did notice a difference between my parents and his— in particular, his mother's dominant nature. For example, one day, we took Norman on a quick visit down the Riccarton to show him our favourite swimming spot by the banks of the Black Devon. While paddling about in the shallows, Norman had picked up a small spot of mud on his trousers. As soon as we got home and entered the sitting room, his mother spotted it at once and immediately reprimanded him. I looked across at my mother and she just looked at me and smiled.

Occasionally, on those rare visits to our part of the world, Norman would be left to spend a day with us while his parents went off to check in on other relatives. I remember one particular warm summer's day, we decided to go swimming at one of our favourite spots: the Peppermill Dam near Tulliallan. It also had an island close to the bank and was easily accessible by just paddling across. It was our Treasure Island.

When we arrived at the location, we took off our shoes and socks and began wading across. About halfway there, I said something like: 'Look out for leeches Norman.' Suddenly, there was this crashing sound of water behind me. I turned and saw Norman back on the bank checking out his legs. When I asked him what the problem was, he said he was a little concerned about *leeches*.

I was informed later that Leeches in his part of the world were a much greater problem than here in Scotland.

## An American Pays a Visit

Our first day back at school was filled with curious excitement. It was the day the exchange teacher from the United States was due to take up her new post in our school.

From the playground, we heard some of the kids call out: *"Here she is!"* We all rushed up and stood on the perimeter wall holding onto the iron railings. We immediately caught sight of this colourful looking person crossing the road accompanied by the Headmaster and some of the other teachers. She was a tall slim built woman with dark hair. She wore an ankle length skirt flared out like a bell tent, and her spectacles looked as if they had wings jutting out from the top edges. Apart from the style of her clothing, the thing that struck me most about them was their bright colours.

As she passed through the playground gate, one of my classmates called out: 'How was your voyage over Miss?' She replied in the expected accent: 'It was swell, thank you.'

Everything about this term was so new, not only getting an exotic teacher, but also the fact that our next classroom was upstairs. The actual physical process of ascending the broad stone staircase to our next classroom felt that we were moving on in life, taking that next step towards adulthood.

As usual, we sat anywhere while waiting to be placed in the assigned seats according to our scholastic achievements. Our new teacher sat on the high chair behind her desk and waited until we all settled in.

She began by introducing herself: Miss Adele Facinelli. Her very name seemed to cause a bit of amusement throughout the whole class. Her surname sounding like the adjective *fascinating* added another dimension to this interesting character.

She had sailed on the SS United States, the fastest ocean-going liner at that time, launched only a year or so before. Her home in America was in Charleston, West Virginia. After her short introduction, she asked us if we had any questions … There was a barrage: had she met any famous Hollywood Stars; were there many Red Indians still roaming the prairies; and what about the gangsters in Chicago?

For the next few weeks, she was the talk of the town. Even her method of discipline took us by surprise. Apparently, she did not believe in corporal punishment … this term was promising to be a most enjoyable experience for all; especially we who were the most vulnerable—the rascals, the cheeky, and the lazy.

However, although initially her method of dealing with us seemed a bit soft and weak, it soon had the same effect. The first lad to receive the new method was Ian Reid; charged with annoying one of the girls, or just talking too much. He was given one hundred lines, something like: *I must not talk during class unless asked to do so*. My turn followed shortly after. At first, I didn't take it too seriously and returned to school next day telling the teacher that I hadn't got around to doing the lines. She promptly gave me an extra one hundred lines on top of the other hundred, and added that failing to have the results on her desk next morning would mean a visit to the headmaster. That outcome was too awful to contemplate, and I soon accepted the new arrangement without any further nonsense.

The agony of sitting at home writing the same sentence over and over again while my pals were outside enjoying themselves could almost be compared to a couple of strokes with the leather strap across the palm of the hands—at least that punishment was over in seconds, and the pain only lasted a minute or so.

Nevertheless, life in Miss Facinelli's class was interesting, and I found myself taking a real interest in certain subjects.

But then one day, shortly after the start of the new term, the headmaster paid a visit to our classroom. He announced that there were going to be some changes made that would involve moving some of us into another classroom. The selected few would be the students who fell below certain standards.

It seemed odd that the new idea was focused only on our class. Was this an attempt to hide the classroom failures from the American guest?

The headmaster readout the names and I found myself one of the chosen. We were moved to a classroom next door for the supposed purpose of concentrated scholastic effort. My new teacher was brought in from *God knows where*, and life took on a completely new status. Suddenly, there I was, separated from classmates that I had known from the very first day at school. I finished up in a room with kids who had so-called learning difficulties. In fact, for the first time in my scholastic experience, I ended up top of the class—without even trying.

The feeling of rejection lasted several days. However, I gradually settled in. The upside of it was, our new teacher, Mr Grant, had a very interesting and outlandish personality. He was this wildly flamboyant man with a vast range of curious characteristics. Often I would sit at my desk with the impression that I was actually watching a scene from one of our local town hall pantomimes.

He was an over-the-top eccentric and possibly gay—although at that time, we had no idea of such things. Even the way he punished us was done with style. If I had learned anything from Mr Grant's class, it was the essence of theatre, especially theatre of the absurd. The very tone of his voice immediately captured your attention—which reminds me of a funny encounter I had with him when on a shopping trip with my mother in Alloa. As we wandered through the Co-operative furniture department, I caught sight of him purchasing something, and as the girl behind the counter asked him for his Co-op share-number, he replied in a cheery high pitch tone: '*The Battle of Hastings.*'

School actually began taking on a strange element that resembled fun. I must say, I rather enjoyed his method of teaching, and I did improve in some things—or was that just my imagination.

For the first time, I was made aware that I was somewhere below the average kid at school. At the time, it didn't concern me unduly. I disliked school and was never made aware of the benefits of a good education. My strong points were art, especially sketching. Reading and writing was about average; however, I found picking up a book and attempting to wade through to the end a bit tiresome, and a dreadful waste of precious time. Generally, I gave up about the middle of the second chapter. My love for reading would come later.

Sums were about average; maybe a bit below, although I was to surprise everyone in later years when I took an interest in amateur radio. Getting involved in practical projects made me aware of the benefits of maths and algebra. I actually took a correspondence course and ended up grasping the fundamentals, especially algebra. Simultaneous equations became my forte.

It was during my term in Mr Grant's class that I first expressed an interest in a job other than the usual things like *train-driver* or *bus-driver*. It came to me when I was invited indoors to watch a programme on a neighbour's TV. The program was about the making of a cartoon show and I decided that that would be the way to go—a cartoon animator!

I told my parents and closest friends that when I leave school, I will journey to California and seek work as an animator in the Walt Disney Studios … That met with uncontrollable mirth and heaps of ridicule. Our small town just couldn't cope with such ludicrous ambitions. No, it looked like I was destined for the coalmines, or something just as mundane. However, the thought of eventually running away to greener pastures never left me.

## Dounans Camp

The months passed by and eventually, the festive season was once again upon us. My Christmas present had been a small two-man tent, and I spent that winter setting it up in the back garden; of course, the weather was far too cold to attempt staying out overnight. That idea would be put off until summer.

Meanwhile, as springtime approached, the school announced that they were taking names for anyone interested in spending a month at Dounans Camp, located just outside Aberfoyle, Stirlingshire. Of course, both my brother John and I wanted to be in on that—a whole month away from school sounded like great fun.

A few weeks before we set off, there were things my mother had to do in preparation for the long stay away from home. The school gave each of us a list of items we should take along with us. Things like several pairs of socks, a couple of shirts and so on. Also, each item had to have a name tag sewn on it. The school supplied the ID tags. It was emphasised that this was not a holiday. There would be classes held each day. Some people compared the experience to a sample of what boarding school might be like.

We arrived at the camp by bus and taken directly to our accommodation. The timber huts were similar to army barracks with double bunk beds spaced out along each side. Our barrack roommates were lads from various schools around the County.

When it came to choosing where to sleep, I was hoping for one of the top bunks. As it turned out, one of my classmates, Ian Reid, was picked to share the same bunk. We tossed a coin to see who would get the top one. Ian won, but he promised to swap over halfway through our stay. Once we had settled in, we began checking out the place. I didn't know it at the time, but apparently, it was a prisoner of war camp. It certainly looked like a military setup.

Later in the evening, a bell rang for supper. The dinning hut was quite big with trestle type tables placed along several rows. Our supper was a couple of bits of toast and a mug of cocoa. After supper, it was back to our hut.

As we prepared for bed, a woman teacher, who was assigned our barrack room supervisor, asked if we would like her to read a bedtime story. We couldn't have been more pleased. There were several books in her room at the end of the hut, and each night she would read from one of them.

Apparently, it was a different set up with my brother John. His hut supervisor was a man, and a strict disciplinarian. Each morning, they had to fold their blankets army-style and place them at the end of their beds. Then after breakfast, they had to return and make the beds.

After the first few days, when the homesickness eased and the novelty wore off, boredom gradually set in. Time spent in the classroom, for example, was a bit erratic: nine thirty starts, two-hour dinner breaks, and half day off on Fridays. This was fine if it were back home among our own familiar environment, but being locked up in a camp surrounded by a high wire fence took its toll.

It seemed we had one activity per week. The first week was the climb up the nearest hill in the Menteith Hill range. The hill itself was covered with thick pine trees, and the trail up to the top was anything but spectacular. As soon as we reached the small rescue hut at the top, it was back down in time for dinner.

Occasionally, they would organise a film night in the large assembly hall. The films generally were a bit dull; documentary types like, *Nanook of the North*, or something similar. There was one adventure story about a couple of lads on the trail of some baddies; but, just as the story was reaching its climax, the film projector went bust and the show was cancelled.

The following week was the march into Aberfoyle to see the famous Poker Tree. The poker hanging from the tree is a historical relic which was used by a character called, Bailie Nichol Jarvie during a confrontation with Rob Roy.

After a moment of staring at the relic, I heard the sounds of laughter from over the road. I looked across and spotted several of our teachers sitting around a table enjoying a couple of cocktails outside a local pub. The boisterous merriment with the occasional outbursts of laughter sounded like they already had more than one.

The boredom got so bad that the girls put together a song sung to the tune of, *One Man and His Dog*. During the last couple of weeks, you could hear throughout the whole camp, their lament …

*Ten more days to go, ten more days of sorrow, ten more days at Dounans Camp, and off we go tomorrow.…*

The following day would be: *"Nine more days to go ..."* and so on until the last day when we were all sitting in the bus with only a few more minutes to go.

## Our First TV

The year 1954 was the year we eventually got our very first television set. It had a beautiful polished timber cabinet with two doors opening out to reveal a fourteen-inch screen. Ma and Dad had bought it from the Alloa Store. They kept it a secret until it was installed.

When I arrived home from school, I couldn't help notice the odd expression on my mother's face. She pointed towards the living room without saying anything. As soon as I saw it sitting in the corner of the living room, I got so excited, I immediately switched it on.

However, the problem was, back in those early days, television programmes only came on at certain times of the day. First up were the programmes for infants: *Bill & Ben, Andy Pandy, Muffin the Mule,* and *Rag Tag and Bobtail,* which started at four o'clock and finished about quarter past four. By the time we got home from school, it was all over. The next viewing times started at five o'clock: Children's Hour. That first day we sat around the set and waited ... and waited, switching it on and off to make sure we didn't miss anything.

From the moment television arrived in the house, our whole way of life altered. Our evening tea moved from the kitchen table to the living room, with our plates balanced on our laps. The large square table in the middle of the living room had to go to clear the viewing area, and my mother found some peace and quiet from the usual racket of noisy kids running up and down. We soon settled into the *cathode-ray tube stare.*

At first, we watched everything from Children's Hour to the Epilogue. The *Grove Family* was my favourite, followed by the increasing BBC plays, such as: *The Railway Children, The Black Arrow,* and of course Johnny Morris as *The Hot Chestnut Man.* We even watched some art programmes like opera, ballet, and Mortimer Wheeler's discussions on archaeology. For the next few months, the whole topic of conversation was based on what was on the TV the night before, or what were the coming attractions. The picture houses in Alloa were starting to feel the pinch.

# Miss Maccowan Loses Her Calm

Meanwhile, back at school, Miss Facinelli had returned to the States, and I was back with my mates in a new class with our new teacher: Miss MacCowan. She was a woman with slightly rounded proportions, and a motherly disposition. Although not too old, her hair was almost all grey. I found her quite pleasant and not too threatening. There was one particular incident in the classroom that left me with a lasting impression of her good-nature.

It was a late summer's day and we were all busy doing something in our jotters. A bumblebee had entered the room and began randomly buzzing about from desk to desk. At first, we paid no attention until one of the lassies got a wee bit excited. It hovered around her head and she tried shooing it away with her jotter. Miss MacCowan reprimanded the lass for being silly and told her there was no need to get excited.

The bee then moved off and started pestering someone else in the room. The whole class began to get a bit agitated, and the noise levels gradually increased. This got Miss MacCowan stirred up and she put her foot down by way of smacking the top of her desk with the blackboard pointer.

As she attempted to restore order, the bee ended up on her shoulder. Someone called out: 'Miss! Miss! It's on your shoulder! It's on your shoulder!' Miss MacCowan suddenly stood quite still and said, 'It's all right … It's all right. Everyone stay calm! There's no need to get excited.' She went on to explain in a calm and responsible manner that a state of panic would only frighten the poor insect and that may cause it to sting.

Meanwhile, the bee had moved onto her neck … this was beginning to look like an insect with a mission, and without further hesitation, it disappeared down the front of her blouse.

The sudden change from complete composure to something resembling a severe bout of *Saint-Vitus-Dance* took over. She jumped up and down shaking her blouse vigorously, and finally she made for the door. She hurried down the corridor as quickly as she could, and disappeared into the staffroom.

Sometime later, she returned and continued her duties as if nothing had happened … I guess we all learned something about bumblebees that day … they are not to be trusted!

# Swimming Lessons at the Baths

Around this time, part of the school activities now involved swimming lessons. On the particular day, we would be transported by bus to the Public Swimming Baths in Primrose Street, Alloa. The girl's session was on the Wednesday afternoon, and ours was a Friday. I was glad we had the Friday slot because it gave the impression that we were given an extended weekend.

When we arrived at the baths and changed into our costumes, the first thing on the agenda was the lesson; which consisted of jumping into the shallow end, hanging on to the side rail, and kicking our feet in the water as if swimming on the spot. The person in charge of us was a woman with a voice that sounded constantly angry, like a female sergeant major. Her shouts bounced off the water and echoed throughout the whole enclosure.

Fortunately, these lessons didn't take up too much time, and we were left to play about by ourselves for the remainder of the day. I was lucky to have mastered a type of swimming technique just a year or so before, so I used the opportunity to try other things like diving of the board. At first, I jumped off the steps, progressing up to the high board.

When it came to diving, things were a wee bit different. I hadn't mastered the right technique. I always seemed to hurt my head when I struck the water, so I gave away the diving and stuck to swimming.

Among the school's activities at the Alloa baths, were the races. For the lads able to swim the full length of the baths, a system was created to determine who the best were. To my surprise, I was consistently in the top three. The best out of my age group was Jim MacMillan from Garden Terrace. I came second, followed very close behind me was PC Kettle's youngest son, Ross.

On the last week of the term, a competition was organised. The prize to each of the first three was a free season ticket to the Alloa Public Baths for a whole year. On the day of the final, I stood nervously at the edge of the pool waiting through the noise of screaming kids for the teacher's: *"Get ready ... Get set ... Go!"* Suddenly, on the command, we were off.

My style of swimming was quite basic. First it involved the belly flap dive, a dive that hit the water without sinking too deep. This saved a bit of time by getting on with the race rather than wasting time resurfacing. From then on, I kept my head down and heard nothing but the dull splashing of my own limbs in the water. Trouble was, I had never mastered the art of breathing without losing the forward motion. It was a case of holding my breath for as long as possible. I would actually get about three quarter way up the length of the pool before taking a breath; but this method left me gasping causing me to pause a bit and loose precious time. Next thing I knew, my hand was on the end rail and I had finished. I felt sure I had lost, and was surprised to find out that I just beat Ross for second place by a hand.

# Chapter 12
# The Last Days at Clackmannan School:
# The First Camping Expedition

The summer holidays before the start of my last year at Clackmannan Primary School were spent doing the usual things, like playing in and around the plantation, or swimming up in the Ladywood. Now and then we'd take along a couple of sandwiches, usually just bread and jam, and maybe a billycan for brewing—or should I say, stewing some tea.

Our billycans were small tin cans with a piece of wire pierced through the rim so that we could suspend them over the campfire to boil up the river water. Two or three broken matchsticks were placed in the boiling brew to curtail the taste of smoke in the finished result … it never did work. Still, it did sound like a good tip from a long forgotten old sage. There were quite a few wee tips and remedies like that; gems of wisdom passed down from generation to generation.

It was around this time that we started thinking of camping out overnight. The campsite was generally the spot beside the Cherryton Brickworks. It was quite a grassy area back then. The only small drawback was fetching water for the billycans. It meant walking down under the main Alloa/Dunfermline railway line viaduct and into the Ladywood.

*Our camping spot beside the Ladywood...*

Just before setting off on the first expedition, my mother packed a few sandwiches and placed them in my kitbag along with some tea and sugar. A drop of milk accompanied this in something like an empty cough mixture bottle. We then headed off for the start of our adventure.

There were six of us altogether; however, two lads had decided not to stay the whole night. That left me, my brother Andrew, Wullie Hill from the Terrace, and George McQueen from Kersegreen Road. Wullie's brother, Stewart, and my brother John, were the temporary company.

When we arrived at the spot, we were surprised to see one of our schoolmates there. Wee Geordie Solomon from Zetland Street. He was sitting round an already lit campfire. He got word of our plan and decided to join us. When I told him there wouldn't be enough room in our small tent, he immediately put our minds at rest with his usual cheery spirit. He turned and pointed to some objects lying beside him. An old car bonnet that he had dragged all the way from Geordie Gray's yard. He explained that by using a couple of suitable tree branches stuck in the ground and placing the bonnet against them, it would act as a kind of lean-to. A blanket would then be draped over the opening giving him—as he thought—sufficient shelter from the night air.

I was, to say the least, a bit doubtful, and a bit curious. I got the impression that he hadn't given much thought to the fact that we were planning on sleeping

176

out here all night; especially when he showed us what he brought for his supper … a bag of sherbet. Anyway, his genuine enthusiasm and pleasant nature turned the whole evening into a kind of party. We soon had the tent pitched, and placed more logs on the fire.

While foraging for more firewood, we approached a signal box beside the main railway line and noticed the signalman leaning over the railings at the top of the stairs. At first, he just stood there smoking his pipe, and casually observing our activities. Then Wullie called out: 'Hello Mister! That looks like a great job you've got there!' He looked down at Wullie, took one puff from his pipe, let go a quick spit from the side of his mouth, and replied casually, 'Aye, it's no bad.'

Wullie kept the conversation going with all sorts of questions like: will he be staying all night, and will there be many trains passing here, and what was it like inside the signal box? Then to our surprise, he invited us all up to have a look.

The first thing we noticed was the row of levers running almost the full length of the interior. They looked like very large brake levers similar to the ones you see on the buses, only much bigger. These, he explained were used for changing the points and various signals along the tracks. I immediately asked him how he knew which one to change. He attempted to explain but it sounded too complicated for me to take in.

Moments later, a bell sounded, and he began the process of pulling one lever, then another. It certainly looked a very relaxing way to spend the working day, but at the same time, it must get very lonely out here with only the sounds of the woodland and the occasional bell clanging. However, he mentioned that it suited his temperament, and that he spent most of the time reading.

Meanwhile, daylight was beginning to fade and we all sat around the campfire spinning yarns and singing songs. Wullie had one particular song that he kept singing. It was one of the latest Judy Garland songs heard on the radio. The pace was slow and dreary and he kept singing the same verse repeatedly until we pleaded with him to stop, but to no avail. Every five or ten minutes, out it would come …

*The night is bitter,*
*The stars have lost their glitter,*
*The winds grow colder,*
*And suddenly you're older*
*And all because of*
*The man that got away ...*

The slow depressing delivery of that verse created an atmosphere about the campsite of gloom and pending discomfort. As the twilight gradually descended into darkness, the night did feel a little bitter and the air a bit cooler; however, the stars lost none of their glitter. We placed the last of our sticks on the fire and sat around watching the dying embers. One by one, we eventually retired to the tent, and wee Geordie disappeared into his makeshift shelter.

Our first experience at camping out over night was a bit of a disaster. Although the day had been a warm one with the temperature up around the seventies, it never occurred to us for a moment that we would feel cold during the night. We were completely ignorant of the fact that, though the day had been warm, and the ground appeared dry, the green grass and the earth beneath was full of moisture. There was one small item missing from our kit that would have made all the difference: a ground sheet. The discovery regarding the benefits of this item would come a year or so later during our involvement with the Boy Scouts.

In addition to that little problem, the cool night air found its way in under the rim of the tent and added to the discomfort. We spent the first half hour or so trying to find a good position on the lumpy ground. Eventually, the eyes got heavy and some of us dozed off for what seemed like only minutes, then the first bite of cold brought us back from dreamland. We rolled about trying to get as much heat as possible by squeezing into each other and fighting for the middle spot so that the others acted as a barrier against the intruding cool night air.

Suddenly there seemed to be a bit of a commotion happening outside. Something was fumbling about with the tent flaps. Then we heard a couple of muffled curses ... it was wee Geordie. He managed to squeeze his head through and pleaded with us to let him come in. As we were all a bit crushed together trying to keep warm, it now seemed that there was more than enough room in the tent for at least another couple; the more the merrier ... so we used him as a wind barrier.

The hours passed, and every now and then, we drifted off only to be woken up by someone rolling about. The bodies lying around the edges fared worse, and they in turn kept the bodies in the middle awake.

Eventually, the faint glow of dawn settled on the white canvas of the tent. The first sound of the dawn chorus gradually increased and resounded throughout the surrounding trees and bushes. The morning light continued to build, and we gave in to the fact that there was no point in trying to grab more sleep. We began blathering about this and that until eventually, one by one, we crawled out to greet the early dawn.

The ground was covered with glistening dew. The sun was still hidden just below the horizon, its glow silhouetting the outline of the brickworks and the old coal-bing of the now defunct Tulligarth coalmine; the mine I had visited all those years before.

I looked over towards the signal box beside the railway. It seemed quiet and lifeless, nothing stirred through the windows. Had the signalman dropped off to sleep, or did he finish his shift hours before? I must admit, I heard no sound of trains passing in the night.

Andrew and Wullie had entered the wood and returned with a small bundle of firewood. We boiled up a billycan and sipped the black stewed tea to warm our insides. After a while, we took a guess at the time and decided to pack up and head for home. Our mothers were not surprised to see us back so early. We had a quick bowl of porridge drenched with hot milk and went straight to bed.

There would be several more camping trips over the summer weeks with the same results. We actually came to expect that that was the norm in the whole experience. However, our provisions did improve a wee bit. We made sure we had enough milk and sugar for our tea, and progress was made in the variety of food. One of the lads actually brought along a chip-pan and some lard. The potatoes were pilfered from one of farmer Norvall's fields, and sometimes even a good supply of broad beans from the adjacent field.

## On to the Control Class

All too soon, our summer break came to an end, and the start of my last year at primary school had arrived. This class was called the Control Class, and as for the new teacher, this was going to be his first engagement at our school. He was

179

replacing Mr MacLean, who took up a new position as Headmaster of Findhorn School in the county of Moray.

Our new teacher's name was Mr Rankin, an ex-British Army officer—so I was told. Strangely enough, he never mentioned his military career all the time I was in his class. He was a fine looking figure of a man who enjoyed sport; especially soccer and cricket. Although I liked playing soccer, it seemed I was never up to the standard for the school team. I actually wasn't too bad in goals and tried to copy the technique of my favourite goalkeeper from the Heart's FC (Wullie Duff); but apparently I wasn't good enough. Dave Meldrum was the lad picked for that position.

Funny enough, I took to cricket OK and became quite a reasonable bowler … I thought. Our first game was against a school in Tullibody. We arrived at a cricket oval situated on the road to Cambus. It was just over the railway line near my older brother John's secondary school: the Alloa Technical. Our captain was Jim Summers, the brightest lad in our class. Jim, like me, was never picked for the soccer team; but cricket seemed to suit him, he even looked the type; the scholastic public schoolboy, more suited to boarding school than our little lot.

He walked over and introduced himself to the captain of the opposing side. Mr Rankin tossed the coin and the other side won, choosing to bat first. For some reason, I didn't perform as well as I should have. Maybe it was seeing the unfamiliar faces of the opposing side that made me nervous, I don't know. I bowled three wides and immediately felt the disappointment from the captain, not to mention the look from Mr Rankin.

Soon, it was our turn to bat and I walked out to the crease still feeling upset with my bowling. I stood at the crease and watched the ball hurtling towards me. I lifted the bat and swung it wildly. The sound of the ball striking the wickets behind sent me into a wee bit of depression. I was out for a duck. I was given a second chance playing against the lads from the bottom end of Alloa, but still my performance was not good enough. I was dropped from the school team from then on.

Life in Mr Rankin's class was, generally speaking, quite interesting. I particularly liked how he introduced projects to support certain subjects. Our geography lesson during this term focused on Australia. I had a particular interest in this part of the world, because my Dad had lived there and never stopped talking about his experiences in that region. He had emigrated during the Great Lockout of 1921. He told us of the time when he first arrived in Melbourne, how he roamed the country as a *Swagman* looking for work around the local farms, and eventually ending up in Queensland working on his own sugarcane farm. He returned to Scotland in 1935 and met my mother; they married the following year. I somehow got the impression, each time he talked of Australia, that he regretted ever leaving the place.

As Mr Rankin began going over the details of the project, his first item on the agenda was getting hold of a very large map of Australia to hang up on the classroom wall. We would then cut and paste clippings from magazines and journals onto the specific areas. He then said that some of us would be assigned the task of drawing the map. I was chosen along with Jim Summers and George Dickson to take charge of drawing this great map.

George was one of the bright lads of the class who had a natural affability and a good sense of humour. Although I never saw much of him during my primary school years, it would be a few years later when we were teenagers. We teamed up along with Cairns Kettles from Kincardine, and Dave McCall from Alloa. Eventually, I was Best Man at his wedding; but that's another story.

There we were, the three of us ushered into a vacant classroom with a very large sheet of paper lying on the floor in front of us. Mr Rankin handed us a book-sized map of Australia and his instructions were to draw the new map eight times the size … The term *eight times* stumped me … what did he mean? Of course, I nodded with sufficient confidence, and immediately looked at the others. Jim began to make a suggestion by demonstrating his method, and George then came up with his own method of approach. By watching and listening to them, the penny dropped … this was going to be a big map.

At first, we had a little difficulty with the size. I was not used to drawing anything on such a scale before and it was clear that the others were having the same problem. When Mr Rankin returned ten or so minutes later, he found us in a bit of a dilemma. Our drawing was not shaping up well. He immediately took a piece of crayon, and in the same energetic style of Rolf Harris, drew the outline himself. Although it was not to scale, it was good enough. We were then left to fill in the details.

Getting involved with practical projects like that gave me a true feeling of satisfaction. If only this method was applied to other subjects, I'm sure it would have made all the difference. The rest of the class did their bit and we completed the whole project successfully. The only problem, as far as acquiring accurate knowledge of a particular region's history, was that we were all led to believe that Captain Cook discovered Australia, where in fact—as I found out much later—it was a Dutchman around the year 1605, one hundred and sixty years before Cook.

There would be many other little anomalies in our education; especially concerning our history. It was not so much that we were told lies, but that many important details were omitted in favour of embroidering Britain's story, and as a Scot, I was saddened to discover that there were many important facts about our own Scottish history that never got a mention.

We seem to be a very proud race of people; and so we should be, but many of us base this pride on myths. How many people in Scotland today know, for example, that *ancestral tartan* was a fairy tale concocted by Walter Scott. James Watt did not invent the steam engine, he invented a component that dramatically improved the already existing steam engine; a component that transformed a primitive device into a machine that would propel the industrial revolution like a rocket into our modern age. The story we got, was a picture of a man sitting by his fireside watching the kettle lid bob up and down, and hitting on the idea of *steam-power*. A bit like the tale of King Alfred and the burnt cakes. I haven't even begun to mention the scores of great Scottish scholars: the philosophers, doctors, engineers, and poets whose contribution played a major part in the whole of our modern society. Meanwhile, we were young and the knowledge was out there. It just takes some of us a little time to wake up.

Back in Mr Rankin's class, the last attempts at turning us into captains of industry (or lieutenants) were being implemented. We were given a sort of trial examination to give us an idea of what to expect on the day of the final exam, which was still quite a few months away.


## Sledging the Braes


The last of the winter snows covered the surrounding district, and sledging down the Fifteen-Acre and Tower Braes was all the go. I still had John Patton's old sledge; the one he gave me when he left for America. It was longer than the usual ones seen around the slopes, which meant I could lay length ways on it without my legs trailing behind. He also left me his bicycle. I was taken completely by surprise when I called on him to say good-bye the day before he sailed. He took me out to the shed at the back of his place in Balfour Street and said something like: 'I'm having a problem fitting these in my suitcase. Would you look after them for me?'

One Sunday afternoon, I prepared the sledge ready for the braes by shining up the runners. Then set off for the first location: the Fifteen-Acre (the local farm worker's term given to a field that runs from the top of the Look-A-Boot-Ye-Brae down to the flat stretches of the Carse).

Although, there was a wire fence at the bottom of the brae, it was a reasonable distance away to be of any concern. In fact, some of us created a competition to see whose sledge would be good enough to reach it. I made several attempts without success, until one day, while on the slopes with a few school pals: Ian Reid, Bert Sharp, Dennis McKeen, and a few others, we began fooling about.

I started at the top of the brae with the rest of the lads piled on top of me. Ian ended up sitting at the back with his feet forward as we set off. Then about halfway down the slope, I noticed that our speed seemed faster than usual; perhaps it was due to the extra weight. Anyway, we hurtled down the brae and kept on going straight towards the fence. The normal practise in times of trouble was to dig your foot in the snow and broadside. However, my legs were pinned down by Ian sitting on them. Some of the lads on top of me realised the problem and began rolling off, but by the time the last one was off, it was too late, disaster was imminent. I kept my head down as much as I could.

I shot through under the fence, just clearing the bottom run of wire and ended up a few yards further on. Ian, on the other hand, didn't fare so well. The wire fence picked him up from the back of the sledge and catapulted him backwards, dumping him on the snow like a rag doll. After a moments silence, everyone ran towards him to see if he was OK. He was soon up and laughing, which set the whole lot of us bouncing about in fits of laughter.

Apparently, the wire had missed his face catching only his stomach and chest. Wearing lots of warm clothing gave him that extra protection. He looked across at me and said, 'Looks like we won the competition.'

After that little bit of excitement, we decided to move on towards the Tower Braes. The slope at the Tower Brae was not for the faint hearted. Not only was the incline steep, it also didn't level out as it did at the Fifteen Acre. The brae continued through a fence and into the Back Wood. This meant you had to acquire a good braking technique. I had mastered the method a year or so before after my brother John's demonstration on the gentler slopes. The trick was to stick out your leg and dig your boot into the snow while forcing the sledge to turn broadside. I had witnessed several nasty accidents with some lads careering straight through the fence and ending up among the trees.

On our arrival at the tower, we saw an unusual sight. Three people on skis. This was something new to us … very exotic. When we got a bit closer, we recognised them at once. It was Mr Rorrison, the ice-cream man, with his son and daughter. Mrs Rorrison was most likely at home minding their small ice cream and sweetie shop at the corner of Castle Street and the Cattle Market. We never had much to do with them—socially that is. They were in this other class of people that we rarely saw much of—middle class you might say; owing to the fact that they were in business. Their daughter was in my class at school. All those years in the same class and I can't remember even having a brief chat with her. There she was, on the slopes of the Tower Braes, dressed up like an Alpine Nordic with a colourful fair isle patterned jumper and a knitted bonnet tied closely round her ears.

Apart from their little shop at the top of Castle Street, Mr Rorrison had an ice cream round. Often we would hear him approach long before he appeared. He had a distinctive rhythm to his pea-whistle. No matter where you were in town, you never failed to recognise that unique sound.

However, competition appeared on the horizon when Neillie Grasso moved his café from the top of Main Street to his brand new premises in Castle Street, just opposite the McAinshs' smallholding. It was a magnificent building in the style of an Italian villa, exterior walls painted white with doors and window frames painted blue. The whole top floor was their accommodation. The new café below had a spacious restaurant and chippery with ample room for storage.

Then, Neillie began his new venture. The start of his ice cream delivery. This was a blow to Mr Rorrison. To begin with, Neillie's ice cream tasted much creamier, and on top of that, he and his wife Flora, both had a genuine warm friendly nature. Anyway, Mr Rorrison survived the strong competition, for they were still trading, even after I had left to seek my fortune in distant lands, some ten or so years later.

## Last Days of Primary School

The last couple of months in Mr Rankin's class were fairly intense with all the preparations for the main exam. However, we did have time to take on interesting little projects, like writing to pen pals in America. Some of the letters

I received looked quite impressive; not so much the content, but their jazzy looking envelopes, and colourful stamps. We, on the other hand sent our replies by aerogramme. It appeared that money was no problem to our American cousins; in fact, I remember receiving an envelope where the post office missed cancelling out one of the stamps, so I carefully removed it and sent it back on the next post … He never replied to thank me.

I suppose being brought up through the rationing years, we developed a healthy respect for the merits of thrift and economy … Well, at least our family did. It often used to annoy me why other kids got interesting toys and we had to settle for much less. It never occurred to me at the time that some families were always up to their ears with hire-purchase debt. My father and mother were very strict on those issues. Then, of course, some of our pals were the only child in the family.

At last, the time had come for our final exam and I had never been through anything so strict. We were all kept apart as much as possible to prevent any likelihood of cheating. The atmosphere in the classroom was so oppressively quiet. No one spoke. An official looking man with a seriously gaunt expression about his face, and a posture resembling that of a tall thin character in a Charles Dickens novel took charge of the proceedings. Nerves got the better of me. I was reading the same question repeatedly and getting nowhere. Instead of moving on to the next question and returning later to the problem ones, I just sat staring down at the seemingly unsolvable. Time was running out and the discomfort stayed with me right to the end. I handed my paper in knowing I could have done a bit better. Anyway, it was all over and gradually everything was back to normal. We all filed out into the playground and the fresh air lifted my spirits enough to dismiss the whole episode as just another day.

Then word got out that a brand new secondary school was being built somewhere near Sauchie. A name had already been chosen: Forebraes Secondary. In a way, it was a bit sad that I would not be joining my older brother down at the Alloa Technical. However, the anticipation of entering this brand new school got us all excited.

A week or so before the last day of term, Mr Rankin stood beside his desk and called out the names of the prize-winners. The top two names were of course, no surprise: Christine Ramsay and Jim Summers, followed by a few others—but then came the shock. I had won another book prize for art and handwork. The announcement, like the last one several years ago, caused a ripple of pleasantries from some of my pals. Once again, my spirits were lifted, sending the trauma of the final exam clear out of my mind.

The handwork was a small woollen scarf in the Heart's team colours. It was woven on a small box frame with a comb and shuttle. Unlike the last book prize where I was presented with Dean Swift's tale of *Gulliver's Travels*—like it or not—this time I was asked to choose my own. Without too much hesitation, I said that I wouldn't mind Robert Louis Stevenson's book, *Kidnapped*. This choice of book took Mr Rankin completely by surprise. A twelve-year-old lad at the lower end of the classroom choosing one of the classics must have seemed somewhat incongruous. I must admit, I surprised myself. I guess it must have been screened on BBC TV that year, for I did know the story and obviously liked it.

Meanwhile, the last few days before the presentation, preparations were underway for our stage performance. Our class act was a Western style square dance selected by our music teacher. As per our usual music lesson, she would wheel the piano into the classroom and bash out the chosen song. It began with the line: *Promenade Doll, skip-to-Ma-loo, skip-to-Ma-loo Ma darl'in. ...*

The dance routine to accompany this would then be choreographed down at the school's drill hall. Our costumes would be our own cloths: check-shirt, cowboy hankie for the neck, and a cowboy hat, which most of us possessed, or at least could borrow from a pal.

All went reasonably well, except that Ross Kettles and I came in too early on a verse, giving us a very stern look from the music teacher. I wasn't as nervous about picking up my prize this time due to my previous experience, which left only one bad incident concerning my top-prize scarf.

On the last day at school, Mr Rankin brought out the box with all our handwork, and began handing out the woollen scarves according to the nametags attached. However, there seemed to be a problem with the nametags on two of them. They had somehow fallen off. The two tags lying at the bottom of the box bore my name and Ian (Guinea pig) Glen's.

Mr Rankin called both of us out to see if we could recognise our own work. He placed them in front of us, and I could see straight away, which was which. Although Guinea had used the same colours as the one I had, his weaving left a lot to be desired. Out of politeness, I hesitated, but just as I was about to reach down and pick my scarf up, Guinea, as quick as a flash, grabbed mine. He turned without further hesitation and immediately returned to his desk.

I was so stunned that I lost my cool and cried: *"Just a minute!"* But, it was no good, Guinea looked in no mood to negotiate. Mr Rankin just stood there with a helpless look on his face. I walked back to my desk holding on to a heap of Maroon and white wool that was supposed to resemble a scarf.

As I made my way out of the school, I dropped Guinea's scarf into the nearest bin. Poor Guinea … bottom of the class every year … was physically kicked about by Miss Duncan in our first year at school … he had nothing to lose.

My days at old Clackmannan School were a mixture of pleasant and not so pleasant memories. Everyone, I'm sure, has their own story to tell. In fact, I honestly can't recall that very last walk across the playground and out through those big wrought iron gates. I think the whole episode ended with the book prizes up at the town hall … I'm not quite sure.

Then of course, my mind was focused on the long summer break and the brand new addition to our family. My older brother John and Stewart Hill from No.1 had set off to visit one of the farms in the district. They returned, each carrying a Border-Collie pup tucked under their jackets. They were purebreds; in fact, they were both descendants of Moss, the famous Sheepdog-Trial champion. Stewart named his dog Lassie, and John called his after the champion.

From that moment on, Moss was part of the family. We had endless hours of fun taking it out for walks. I was amazed at how quickly it picked up certain commands; in fact, it had its own unique personality. I was sure it could understand every word we said, and it actually had its own sense of humour. It would greet you with a smile, curling up its top lip and showing its teeth. Some people thought it was about to bite, but it was actually smiling at them. In fact, I even caught it sniggering on several occasions, as if it were tittering, or suppressing laughter. For example, it would happen on occasions when it caused a bad smell. We would cry out: *"Oh! Moss! You stink …"* and it would skulk away lowering its head, and then glance back with a little smile and a snigger … its true!

## The Body in the Quarry and Crime and Punishment

As we approached the last week of the holidays, we began speculating on what our new school was going to be like. This would be a whole new experience. For the first time, it meant travelling over 2 miles by special bus all the way to Sauchie.

Then there were the different subjects: woodwork, metalwork, technical drawing, and science. It all sounded interesting stuff. Forebraes Secondary school would be for me the end of my childhood. Even in the very first year, I began noticing changes. One major difference came over me quite unexpectedly. I suddenly got emotionally involved with one of the opposite sex. The age of the adolescent had come upon me with all its embarrassing and silly consequences. No one ever prepared me for this part of growing up, this god-awful state of being half child, half man.

Our small community was also going through some changes; some good, and some not so. A younger heavy framed individual with short red hair and a mean looking round face was replacing PC Kettles. He was convinced that our town was a breeding ground for potential criminals. Catch them young was his policy before they develop into uncontrollable gangsters. He seemed to be around every corner.

One day, while playing inside the tower with my brother Andrew and our pal George McQueen (who incidentally, ended up years later with a career in the police force, holding the rank of Detective Chief Inspector of the Maidstone constabulary in Kent), we spotted Botham and he spotted us. As we tried to make our escape, he was one-step ahead, cutting us off at the pass—to use a Hollywood expression. PC Kettles, who was still on the job, arrived a couple of minutes later.

There we were, standing shoulder to shoulder before these two enormous figures of authority, our heads bowed low, and staring at the ground in a state of total submission. As PC Kettles was in the midst of delivering his sermon on: *"What a song there would be if we fell from such heights,"* a ladybird suddenly decided to take a short-cut across PC Botham's very large boot. Andrew, standing beside me, went into convulsions of uncontrollable chuckling. His shoulders bobbed up and down so much that his condition infected both George and me. We just could not control ourselves. PC Botham was outraged, but PC Kettles just told us sternly that this was no laughing matter and sent us off with a warning.

There were only two occasions where I observed PC Botham looking pleased with himself. The first happened during a tragic event that occurred down the bottom of the Look-Aboot-Ye-Brae.

About one hundred yards from the bottom of the brae was an old disused quarry. It was a small rectangular area about half the size of a football pitch, and surrounded by a fence and a few bushes. The local council and others now used it to tip their rubbish. Over the years, the quarry gradually filled with water, and due to the constant tipping of all sorts of debris, the surface of the water ended up coated with a thick layer of grime; it actually made the surface look solid. That set the scene for the inevitable tragic event.

One day, a truck entered the quarry and began unloading its contents. Then the driver's mate stepped out of the truck and did a bit of rummaging about looking for anything interesting. He apparently saw something that caught his attention. Unfortunately, it sat floating on the thick-coated surface of the water. To him, it looked like solid ground. He stepped out and immediately sank below the grimy surface. He struggled in an attempt to reach the edge but couldn't quite make it due to the amount of rubbish floating on the surface. When the driver of the truck saw him finally disappear under the water, he jumped into his truck and raced off to the nearest public phone box.

I first heard of the tragedy when I arrived home from school. As soon as my mother told me the news, I raced off down to the location. When I reached the bottom of the Look-Aboot-Ye-Brae, I could see in the distance, scores of people, a number of vehicles, and the familiar shape of an ambulance. I reached the spot and stood by looking on.

Paddling about on the surface of the water were two men in a small rowboat. One of them was standing holding a rope with a grappling hook on the end … It was PC Botham. At first, I didn't recognise him dressed in his civvies. I assumed the emergency call caught him off-duty. The other odd thing about him was his jokey manner. He was treating the whole event as if fishing for a prize catch. A short time later, he managed to hook the body. When it came to the surface, he gave a triumphal cry: 'Got Ye!'

I had never seen a dead body before. This was my first experience. As Botham gradually pulled it out of the grimy water, all I could make out was its shape, as if the man had died sitting at the wheel of a car with his hands on the steering and his legs in a sitting position. The whole corpse was completely covered in thick grey looking grime, and as stiff as a board … and there stood PC Botham looking very pleased with himself. I suppose to a policeman, this was just all in a day's work.

In comparison to the now retired PC Kettles, PC Botham was a man with a very different personality, where PC Kettles had this aura of authority mixed with a balance of natural justice, Botham saw bad in all of us. Eventually, we were to meet up over a serious matter, which would be the second occasion where I noticed a faint look of pleasure across his face.

Due to one of my many naive adventures, the inevitable happened. It began as a harmless act of truancy—something I had never done before. It was during my second year at Forebraes School. The bus had brought us all back home for our midday meal. Then, while waiting up at The Cross for the bus to take us back to school, one of my classmates uttered something like: 'What a pity having to spend such a nice day sitting in a classroom.' I don't know which one of us suggested taking the afternoon off, all I know is, it sounded like a great idea.

As we stood on the steps of the old Mercat Cross watching the school bus disappear past Rorrison's corner, and on down the Cattle Market, we set off strolling down the Main Street, stopping for a moment at Stein's chemist shop on the corner of the South Venal. We then entered the Venal and rummaged about behind the old vacant-looking houses next to Jock Russell's electrical storehouse (an uninhabited house in the Main Street he rented to store his cables and switches and the like).

After climbing up a wall next to—what we thought was an empty house next to Mr Russell's place—we noticed a couple of loose tiles around the gutter. When we lifted them up, we could see into the attic. Jim and I looked at each other and began removing a few more.

Soon we were inside the attic and standing over the ceiling access lid. As we lifted the lid, we saw a well-worn carpeted hallway. We lowered ourselves down and moved about opening a door to one of the rooms. To our surprise, we saw that all the rooms were furnished—albeit sparsely. The kitchen drawers had all sorts of basic household items in them. It was as if the place had just simply been abandoned.

The downside was that we were totally oblivious to the seriousness of the situation. This was obviously somebody's home; but—as we later found out—it had been left vacant for well over a year. We were completely unaware of the fact that the occupant was spending their last days in an old people's home.

We finally made our way back into the attic and out the way we came, replacing the tiles. I arrived home with a couple of pots looted from the house. As I presented them to my mother, she started asking a lot of questions. During the *third degree,* I gradually let the cat out of the bag, so to speak. I confessed that I didn't go back to school, and that we had found this abandoned house with all sorts of goodies in it … She shot straight through the roof; I had never seen her so upset. When my Dad came in from work, he also went into a state of mild panic. He took the pots and threw them into the rubbish tip across the vacant lot at the back of our house.

Several weeks past, during which time, other lads got to hear of the old house and inevitably, one got caught. How this particular lad managed to get himself caught, I will never know, and frankly, I don't much care. He just happened to be one of my archenemies, fancied himself as the hard-man of the school bus— not that he was a physical threat to anyone, he was far too weedy looking for that status.

However, as it happened, the police caught him and without much hesitation, he turned Queen's Evidence, naming me as the original culprit. He never mentioned Jim.

Eventually, when I came home from school and entered through the backdoor, I immediately noticed a grim expression on my mother's face. She told me the police wanted a word with me. They sat on the settee in the living room, a plain-clothes policeman and PC Botham. I couldn't get over how small our large settee looked accommodating these two characters. They looked altogether squished and very uncomfortable. They began asking me all sorts of questions. I tried to explain that there was no criminal intent. That Jim and I were only playing. One of them said something like: '… And your friend Jim …' There was a short pause, and he continued with, '… I seem to have forgotten his last name.' I said his name. 'Ah! That's right.' Then he said, 'And he lives at …?' Jim was now involved. We were both charged with malicious damage and sentenced to two years' probation.

As time passed, the realisation that we were no longer innocent children, that we were entering a stage in our lives where we had to take responsibility for our own actions suddenly became apparent. Things we regarded as innocent fun were actually causing distress to some folks. Invading people's gardens to steal apples often involved the destruction of a neighbour's garden. The trampling down of someone's prized roses that took years to nurture. This final silly adventure was, for me, the catalyst. The old penny dropping, so to speak. The difference between a mischievous childish prank and criminal activity was now obvious.

# The Finale

Meanwhile, a new craze in music had suddenly arrived on the scene to lift our spirits. When I first heard the term, *Rock and Roll*, it sounded like the start of a very exciting revolution. The film *'Rock Around The Clock'* with Bill Haley and his Comets, landed in our midst like an unexpected popular guest at a very dull party. Everyone who saw the film—and I don't personally know of anyone at Forebraes school who didn't—immediately took on the style of dancing and the phraseology, like: *"Cool baby,"* and *"Get in the groove, darl'in."* This style of music became ours. The oldies were left behind with their old ways, and their boring ballads. Dad complained endlessly saying that these new songs were just a lot of rubbish; that they were repetitive, and what's more, you couldn't make out a word they were singing. But to us, it was magic, and a few years on, the Beatles arrived. The Sixties was, I suppose, our generation's equivalent of the Roaring Twenties.

Then came the day I left school, April 1958. It actually felt like leaving home for the first time. The week before I left, the careers officer recommended a position with the National Coal Board as a trainee coalminer. It seemed I was fated to join the ranks of the Bevan Boys.

However, as soon as my Dad got wind of this, he immediately took me in to see the General Manager of the Alloa Co-operative at the head offices in Marr Street. My Dad, being an active member of the Union Movement, appeared to have some influence in that society. I was given a choice of three apprenticeships: Furniture Upholsterer, Butcher, or Fishmonger. Of course, I chose Upholstering.

Unfortunately, the day before I was about to embark on this trade, the whole furniture department in Primrose Street burned to the ground. As it happened, I witnessed the whole event.

I had called into J. B. Rae's small bookshop in Primrose Street, directly opposite the public baths. While browsing the bookshelves, I gradually sensed something happening outside in the street. I stepped out onto the pavement to investigate and immediately saw smoke pouring out some of the department store windows. I stood with the rest of the spectators and watched the drama unfold.

The town's eccentric tramp, Wullie Gut, tried to sneak in and nick some of the goods, but he was prevented from doing so due to a policeman standing near-by and calling after him with a very loud roar.

The Alloa fire brigade arrived; but all too soon, the fire spread to other sections of the building. Sometime later, the Stirling brigade arrived with their long ladders; but by that time, the whole building was raging out of control. I stood watching the scene for quite some time, and finally I decided I had seen enough.

On the way home, the question was, what was going to happen now that there was no furniture department? The answer of course was, there would be no new apprentice-ships in that trade until further notice. I had to make a choice between the other two trades.

A few days later, I started work at the butcher shop in Drysdale Street. I wasn't there an hour when Mr Donahue, the branch manager, persuaded me to help out in the fish shop … just until they found a boy to fill the spot … I was there five years.

Then in 1963, I felt that I needed a change. I handed in my notice, much to my parents' disappointment. After packing my bags and saying goodbye to everyone, I jumped on a bus at Edinburgh and landed in Luton, England. I stayed there just over a year.

After returning briefly to work in the Clackmannan Store's grocery department as a van salesman, I met and married a Tullibody girl. In 1965, we both immigrated to Australia where we eventually divorced eight years later.

As an infant, growing up in a small mining town during the post-war period, I consider my childhood years were as rich as anyone's could be. The surrounding countryside was our playground: the Kennet estate, with its stately home, and beautiful old farm building resembling a large Spanish hacienda; the grounds dotted with various old trees; and the rich variety of colourful flowers and wild berries were a constant source of inspiration. Our small community was also endowed with a variety of characters; some humorous, some not so, and quite a few bordering on the eccentric. Apart from the locals, we had the occasional exotic person popping in from distant parts. Every now and then, a Frenchman with that quintessential French beret on his head would show up on a bicycle selling onions. His produce was draped across the handlebars of his bicycle. The locals called him *Ingin-Johnny*. I can't recall my mother ever purchasing any.

Then there was the old tramp with his big scruffy grey beard. He strolled about the streets singing incomprehensible songs. People took such pity on him, and our mothers would give us a penny or two to pop in his hat. He had a typical Highland accent that gave him that extra appeal … It was discovered much later that he was a bit of a fraud. He was actually quite well off with his own property somewhere in Argyllshire.

That particular period of my past will never come back, and I'm sure it's the same with us all when we reach a certain age. However, the dreadful sadness I felt after a recent visit to see the once beautiful grounds of the Kennet Estate now reduced to a dull featureless open field, and the callous destruction of the historic Kennet House was deeply depressing. This was part of our history, the Bruce family residence for nearly two hundred years. Even the town itself is developing into a suburban sprawl. I suppose we just have to accept that things change. But, the question constantly nagging me is: Is it for the better?

A local lad's poem:

William Burns was a Clackmannan lad who wrote a poem of his childhood days in the 1830s:

## Tae Robin, My Schoolmate, Clackmannan

There's mair than thirty years, Robin, Been laid beneath the mool, Sin' we were bairns the gither, Robin, Toddlin' to the schule.

Sin' we stood side by side, Robin, And reverent closed the eye,

And heard the morning prayer, Robin, Addressed to Him on high.

When ither tasks were through, Robin, Ye'll mind it was the rule, To read the Book o' Books, Robin, Ere skailin' o' the schule;

The partin' blessin' gi'en, Robin, We scampered aff wi' glee.

It's been a pleasin' dream, Robin, Through thirty years to me.

The Saturdays you'll mind, Robin, We tasted freedom then, We were nae langer boys, Robin, But mighty huntin' men.

Our breeks were buckled hi', Robin, Till legs and knees were bare, Then bickered o'er the fields, Robin, Playing 'catch the hare.'

Awa' o'er the Bride's Craft, Robin, Wi' lithesome limbs we'd scour, Across the green brae's face, Robin, An' round by the auld tower;

Among the ne'stlin' ivy, Robin, Upon its moulderin' wall,

We'd snugly hide, and hear, Robin, Our comrades' gathering call.

Our pleasures were as keen, Robin, I'll wad a siller groat, As bigger folks that rode, Robin, Dressed in a scarlet coat.

Sae little worth's the crap, Robin, That grows on pleasure's field;
But deeds o' purpose noble, Robin, Gie aye a glorious yield.

Then through the matted hedge, Robin, Wi' peerin' e'en we'd keek, To rob the wee birds' nests, Robin, Our selfish hands would seek.

I trust we've tried since syne, Robin, Mair honest sense to gain, Than gratify oorsel's, Robin, While ge'in' ithers pain.

Whiles doun at the auld cross, Robin, We'd eager ply the game, And jink about the steeple, Robin, Or round the muckle stane.

The peerie whiles we'd spin, Robin, Whiles play at 'buff the boar,' Near deavin' Annie Higgins, Robin, Wi' oor confoundin' roar Whiles playin' at the ba', Robin, Or playin' at 'high spie.'

Whiles quarrellin' o'er the bools, Robin, Wi' dinsome words and high.

Frae laddies men might learn, Robin, Their differences to mend, For war and peace wi' us, Robin, Did aye the gither blend.

The memory o' thae times, Robin, A pleasure aye can gie;
And I hae little doubt, Robin, The pleasure aft you pree.

When sittin' by the ingle, Robin, Cheered wi' its kindly glow, Musin' on the days, Robin, O' thirty years ago.

William Burns, a Clackmannan lad born in 1825. His other poems were: 'The Floweret', 'Friendship's Cure', 'Early Morn in Summer', 'Tae Robin, my Schule-Mate, Clackmannan', 'Daddy, tak' your bairn', 'To the memory of the late William Drummond, Esq, Rockdale Lodge, Stirling', 'Verses addressed to Cambuskenneth', 'Designs', etc.